Cornwall and the
Isles of Scilly
BY A. IVAN RABEY

Polperro

Published by COLLINS Glasgow and London

First Published 1975

*Cover photograph of St. Ives is reproduced by
    permission of* COLOUR LIBRARY INTERNATIONAL

Drawings and map by MIKE JACKSON

Design and layout by RONALD MONGREDIEN

Photographs by courtesy of J. ALLAN CASH *(title page.
    pages 47, 67, 70, 74);* PETER BAKER *(pages 8, 48, 62,
    87, 90);* JEREMY GRAYSON *(pages 17, 52);* ROBERT ROSKROW
    (page 29); J. B. TREMAIN *(pages 36, 54);* JEFF TOTTLE
    (page 50); LOUIS AND DAPHNE PEEK *(page 76).*

ISBN 0 00 434739-6
Copyright © *A. Ivan Rabey 1975*
PRINTED IN GREAT BRITAIN

CONTENTS

INTRODUCING CORNWALL

Ever since the railway came to Cornwall during the 19th century and the famous Cornish Riviera Express first hurtled its way westward across Southern England and over Brunel's mighty bridge into the land beyond the Tamar, simply the thought of going to Cornwall for a holiday has brought pleasure to millions of people from all over the British Isles, and, latterly, from all over the world.

Cornwall attracts a tremendous number of visitors each year, and it is hoped that the reasons for this immense popularity may be found in this book. It is divided into three sections: the first deals briefly with the history, legends, culture and customs, and thus provides the background to a holiday visit. It also gives information on a number of specific topics, such as activity holidays, bus and rail facilities, and caravanning and camping. The second section divides the county into four areas, describes certain holiday and touring centres in some detail and suggests tours, excursions and places to visit. The romantic Isles of Scilly are also described in a separate chapter. A gazetteer of all the principal towns as well as many of the villages completes the third section.

HISTORY, LEGENDS AND CULTURE

The Celtic Heritage. Cornwall is a Celtic country and very proud of it. Its history goes back three thousand years or more to the time when the first visitors came to its shores. These were the Phoenician tin traders who sailed from the Mediterranean across the Bay of Biscay and landed on the remote rocky shores of the Cornish Peninsula in order to barter for tin. Tin was the life blood of Cornwall from those earliest times right down to the great depression of 1869, when, because of the fall in the price of tin due to large finds elsewhere in the world, Cornish miners had to seek their fortunes in such farflung places as Nevada, Montana, Michigan and Peru.

Tin played such an important part in the life of Cornwall that when the mining industry fell upon hard times during the middle of last century it was almost a national disaster. The ruins of the mine engine houses, or 'jinjies' as they are called, can still be seen dotted around the bare, open countryside, particularly around Camborne and Redruth, gaunt reminders of the days when Cornwall was very much an industrial county.

At the time the Phoenicians were coming to the shores of Cornwall, the Cornish were living in very primitive conditions. Their earliest habitations were similar to the 'bee-hive' village of Chysauster, near Penzance, or the coastal forts such as Porth Island, near Newquay, or the hill-forts on the conical hills which dominate the uplands and moors of inland Cornwall, such as Castle-an-Dinas on the Goss Moor. These interesting places can still be visited and further mention will be made in subsequent chapters.

The Celtic Saints. The next visitors to Cornwall brought Christianity. Holy men and women, mainly from Southern Ireland, left their mark in the strange sounding names of the towns and villages. Foremost among these saints was **St. Petroc** who is associated with the great church at Bodmin which bears his name, with Padstow (or Petrocstow) and Little Petherick or St. Petroc Minor. Another was **St. Piran** whose Oratory, probably the oldest surviving place of Christian worship in Cornwall, lay buried in the sand for generations, but is now preserved in a concrete shell. St. Piran gave his name to Perranporth and the surrounding parish of Perran-zabuloe, whilst the story of **St. Neot,** whose church lies just off Bodmin Moor, and contains the finest examples of Medieval stained glass to be found in Cornwall, is well worth the telling.

St. Neot, it appears, had a well in which there were three fishes, and in a vision he received divine permission to catch and eat these fish pro-vided that at any time he did not take more than two. It so happens that St. Neot was taken ill and a neighbouring holy man came to visit him. This visitor thought that St. Neot could do with a good meal so he took all three fish from the well, cooked them and set them before St. Neot who quite naturally was horrified. He immediately shot up from his pallet and popped all three fish in their cooked state back into the well. To his delight and relief they all started to swim around again quite happily, thus providing a miracle and ensuring the continuation of his supply of fresh fish.

Apart from St. Petroc, St. Piran and St. Neot, St. Columba, St. Morwenna, St. Agnes, St. Eia, St. Austell and many more are still vene-rated among the saints who brought the Christian Gospel to Cornwall.

Perhaps the most tangible reminder of these earliest times are the standing stones, dolmens and menhirs which can be found scattered throughout the length and breadth of the county. Well over 400 stone monoliths or crosses, which form a complete subject for study in them-selves, marking the places where the Saints preached or the crossing places of moorland tracks, can still be visited, as can the great stone circles of the Merrymaidens near Penzance, the Hurlers high on Bodmin Moor, and the massive remains of burial places of chieftains as at Lanyon Quoit near Ludgvan.

Even at Newquay, Cornwall's largest and most modern holiday resort, reminders of the older civilisations linger on. The large open space of the Barrow Fields overlooking the sea at Narrowcliff takes its name from the earthen barrows, or tumuli; the burial places which are to be found all over the county and particularly in coastal fortified areas.

The Saints also left their holy wells, about one hundred in all, each with its own particular virtue or miracles. Some of these wells have long since disappeared, for example, **St. Columba's Well** at Ruthvoes, where only the merest trickle of water survives to give credence to the story. Others, by contrast, are well-preserved with splendid medieval granite canopies or chapels—these are mentioned in the appropriate later chapters as places of interest to visit. The special cures or miracles attaching to some of the holy wells are interesting, in that they reflect the horror with which certain ailments, now accepted by modern medical science as comparatively minor, were then regarded. Drinking or being immersed in the waters of St. Piran's Well at Perranporth was reputed to be an efficaceous cure for rickets, whilst St. Mawes' Well had curative properties over worms, and St. Cubert's Well, which was accessible only at low tides, was infallible in cases of skin disease.

Legend and Folklore. After the spate of saints and the founding of the Celtic Church in Cornwall, mainly during the 6th century, history and legend continue to be so interwoven that it is often difficult to discern one from the other. Perhaps, however, this shadowy area where fact and fiction merge provides the visitor with the most colourful and interesting picture of ancient Cornwall.

The Cornish version of the Arthurian legend, centred on Tintagel Castle on the rocky north coast, makes fascinating reading in **Tennyson's** *Idylls of the King*. Place names such as Camelford (Camelot) and Slaughter Bridge (where **King Arthur** was finally defeated and slain) or Tremodrett (Mordred's Town) and Domellic (Domellioc) on the Goss Moor (the King's reputed hunting-ground) all add substance to Cornish claims to King Arthur's sovereignty.

The Mermaid of Zennor. Another ancient story concerns the parish of Zennor in the far west of the county. Here legend has it that one day a mermaid swam ashore and became infatuated with the sweet singing of one Matthew Trewhella, a member of the church choir. The mermaid too had a lovely voice and on Sundays she used to sit out in the church yard and join in the singing. Matthew Trewhella was soon captivated by her singing and one day he could stand it no longer. He rushed from his place in the choir out into the church yard, and hand in hand with the mermaid he plunged headlong into the sea and disappeared beneath the waves. On moonlit nights it is said that one can hear the sweet voices of Matthew Trewhella and his mermaid joined in an eternal duet. That this story is of considerable antiquity is borne out by the fact that in Zennor Church can be seen a beautifully carved bench-end depicting a mermaid complete with her comb and looking-glass and it is given further point by the old nautical superstition and belief that mermaids, or sirens, used to sit on rocks and by their sweet singing lure sailors to their doom.

If legend is too naïve for the sophisticated reader and historical accuracy is needed one can refer to books such as *The Making of the English Landscape: Cornwall* by W. G. V. Balchin, F. E. Halliday's *History of*

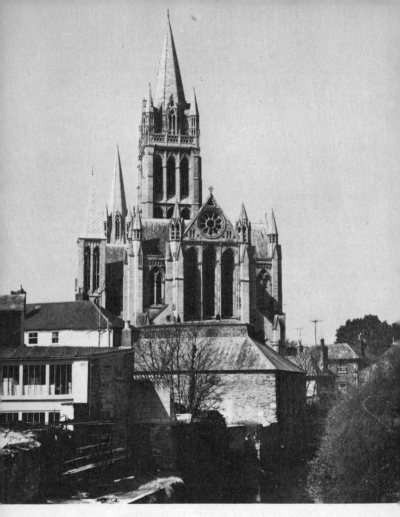

Truro Cathedral

Cornwall or *The Story of Cornwall* by the well-known Cornish historian, A. K. Hamilton Jenkin. Canon G. H. Doble's series of pamphlets on the *Lives of the Cornish Saints* are also very well worth reading.

Cornwall's Churches. In the years following the Norman Conquest, Cornwall was beginning to take on a somewhat different aspect. The great manors such as Bennacott near Boyton in North Cornwall, Hamatethy in the moorland parish of Blisland, Gaverigan in St. Columb parish, Tretheake in Veryan or Kelynack in St. Just-in-Penwith, came into being and were recorded in the Domesday Book. The great church of St. Germans with its splendid Norman doorway ceased to be the cathedral church for the See of Cornwall and was taken over by the Bishops of Exeter.

It was not, however, until the Middle Ages when the majority of churches were built, that readily traceable history now enshrined within their walls began to take shape. These Cornish churches, built by a variety of benefactors, nobility, landed gentry, traders and merchant venturers, deserve more than just a passing glance and are well worth visiting. In the majority of churches excellent leaflets or guide-books can be found, very often incorporating first-rate accounts of local history as well as drawing attention to the architectural features and noteworthy aspects of the building.

Canon Miles Brown, the Vicar of St. Winnow with St. Veep, has published a most detailed and painstaking volume *What to look for in a Cornish Church* which is commended to all interested in this subject. Brief mention of some features of the more notable parish churches is made in the gazetteer, but the list is by no means comprehensive.

Many Cornish churches had Chantries, dissolved between 1545 and 1549, but at the Reformation many Cornish families remained loyal to the Church of Rome, at great personal risk, and financial impoverishment. One such was the important family of Arundell of Lanherne in the parish of St. Mawgan-in-Pydar. Their manor house has been a Carmelite convent since 1794 and remains a centre of Roman Catholicism in mid-Cornwall. Among the relics venerated at Lanherne is part of the skull of St. Cuthbert Mayne, a Jesuit priest who was martyred for his faith in 1577.

The 17th Century. Cornwall also played its part in the Civil War. Many of the county's gentry supported the Royalists and Daphne du Maurier's famous novel *The King's General* is based on the story of Sir Bevil Grenville of Stow near Stratton. Many fierce battles were fought between the Cavaliers and the Roundheads, those at Stamford Hill, Braddock Down and Tresillian Bridge being three important clashes.

The Cornish also did not take kindly to changes in religious worship brought about by the new Prayer Book of **Edward VI,** and later, in 1688, Jonathan Trelawney, once Vicar of St. Ive near Liskeard, was one of the seven Bishops imprisoned in the Tower by **James II** for petitioning against the Declaration of Indulgence. Cornishmen marched towards London reaching Exeter before they heard news of the Bishops' release. This inspired Robert Stephen Hawker, the parson-poet of Morwenstow in a later era, to write the stirring 'Song of the Western Men' which has become 'Trelawney', the Cornish anthem.

The Religious Revival of the 18th Century. As time went on, social and religious matters became even more integrated. By the 18th century far too many clergymen holding important livings in Cornwall, which at that time was an Archdeaconry within the Diocese of Exeter, were non-resident and the scene was set for the religious revival spearheaded by that great evangelist **John Wesley.** Wesley brought a message of hope to the ordinary people and made a great impact, particularly in the mining communities where the public-house was often the only means of social intercourse.

In consequence of this revival 'dissenting chapels' sprang up. Many miners were converted to effective Christianity and became well-loved 'rounders', or itinerant lay preachers, a tradition which proudly survives in Cornish Methodism today.

One such was Billy Bray, who virtually single-handed and between shifts of working below ground in the mines, built the little 'Three-eye' chapel at Twelveheads, near Baldhu, just outside Truro.

The religious enthusiasm which Wesley generated also led to an affection for him personally. One of the features of Methodism in Cornwall was, and still is, hymn-singing, and traditional Cornish carols followed. There was also a tremendous following for the doctrines of total abstinence and an astonishing number of Bands of Hope and Rechabite Tents were founded.

Around 1820 the Reverend William O'Bryan, born at Gunwen, near

John Wesley

Bugle started the Bible Christian movement, known locally as 'the Bryanites', and this denomination, too, was not without its followers. Many corps of the Salvation Army were also founded.

The Railway and the First Tourists Arrive. As Cornwall moved into the latter half of the 19th century the coming of the railway changed the way of life yet again. By 1900 Cornwall was beginning to be 'discovered' as a place for summer holidays and from then on, the influx of tourists has steadily increased until the present day. In 1974, for example, it was estimated that three million visitors came to the county in search of the relaxation and recreation provided by the natural amenities set against the interesting background for which Cornwall has become world-renowned.

The Lure of the Beaches. Wonderful bathing beaches, providing unique facilities for surfing and other forms of water sports, stretch for some 85 miles from Bude and Widemouth Bay, not far from the Devon border, right down to St. Ives, Sennen Cove and finally to Lands End, where ocean meets channel and the sea is in constant turmoil. The location and particular merits or charms of most of Cornwall's beaches will be mentioned later, and merely to catalogue them here would be a pointless exercise. The Atlantic coast is, of course, only half the story. From Lands End the 'west' coast continues southwards along Mounts Bay towards the Lizard—the most southerly point in the British Isles.

The South Coast. Once around the Lizard a noticeable change comes over both seascape and landscape. The waters of the English Channel are more tranquil than those of the Atlantic Ocean unless the wind happens to be blowing strongly from an easterly point. In consequence the land itself is softer, there are more trees, and the vegetation is generally more luxuriant, in places even bordering on the sub-tropical. The calm waters of the Helford River, the Fal and the Fowey provide safe anchorages and yachting, and all forms of 'messing about in boats' is very popular.

The wide sweeps of the Veryan, Gerrans and St. Austell Bays provide unforgettable panoramic views which are mirrored in the glorious stretches of Whitesand Bay as the Cornish coast finally exhausts itself after Rame Head, in the historic waters of Plymouth Sound and the Hamoaze.

One can indulge in all forms of water sports from shark-fishing and skin-diving to Malibu-surfing and water-skiing all around this delightful coast.

The Cornwall Coast Path. For those who wish to see the beauties of the coast at first-hand, without taking to the water, it is possible to walk on the Cornwall Coast Path, which, with only a few minor lengths excepted, now runs all the way round the county.

Inland Cornwall. It has often been said, rather unkindly and certainly thoughtlessly, that Cornwall is a county with a beautiful coastline but an ugly hinterland.

This is definitely not the case, and the misapprehension may have arisen because the pioneers in the guide-book-producing field tended to concentrate on the resorts and coastal areas so much as to almost completely exclude inland Cornwall.

The Little Rivers. Mention has already been made of three of Cornwall's loveliest rivers. To these can be added many more, but the upper reaches of the Camel and the Valency are worth mentioning here because they both rise on the high moors and flow into the Atlantic Ocean. The estuary of the River Camel provides excellent facilities for boating and water-skiing as it passes Padstow with yet more boating and splendid sandy beaches at Rock and its neighbours on the other side.

The beautiful Valency Valley includes that part of Cornwall beloved of **Thomas Hardy,** the West country novelist who was associated with the parish and little church of St. Juliot. The valley ends in a rocky cleft at Boscastle, one of the most attractive of all the Cornish seaport villages.

The Moorlands. Most of Cornwall's rivers rise on the high moors which in themselves are well worth a visit. Even though they lack the grandeur of the Scottish moors and the bleakness of Dartmoor and Exmoor, Bodmin Moor, the Goss Moor and the heights of Goonhilly, Carnmarth and Penwith nevertheless have a fascination all their own.

On these windy uplands can be traced relics of the former civilisations of Cornwall and on a moonlit night it is easy to let the imagination have full play so that the moors come alive with the shades of the Botathen ghost, or of Daniel Gumb, a primitive yet extraordinarily scholarly astronomer. Then there is the Cornish 'Faust', Jan Tregeagle, unjust steward to Lord Robartes of Lanhydrock. Tregeagle sold his soul to the Devil and can only keep him from claiming his part of the bargain by working at impossible tasks such as emptying with a leaky limpet shell the 'bottomless' Dozmary Pool on Bodmin Moor (the legendary resting-place of Excalibur, the sword of King Arthur), or fleeing from the Hounds of Hell to seek sanctuary in the former anchorite's cell and chapel on the top of Roche Rock.

Villages. Hidden among the wooded valleys of the rivers and dotted around the fringes of the moors one finds the small, sequestered rural villages of Cornwall. In the east and north of the county these inland villages are centres of farming and horticulture, whereas to the west of Truro are the mining villages of the last century, whose once despised cottages are now undergoing extensive renovation.

The centres of village life are the church, the chapel, the pub, the village hall (probably built as a memorial after one or other of the World Wars) and, in summer, the recreation ground.

Customs and Markets. In size, the market towns are comparatively small. Boroughs, as a result of local government re-organisation are, alas, no more, but in many places traditions and ceremonies are still observed. At Bodmin the curfew is still rung every night; Helston still has its Furry Dance; Summercourt retains its Fair on September 25th; St. Columb men continue to hurl the silver ball in the main streets of the town at Shrove-tide as did their medieval forefathers, and Padstow's Mayers still maintain the rites of summer by dancing behind their 'Obby 'Oss on May Day, whilst up and down the county, fairs, carnivals, regattas, hey-days, bell-ringing festivals and garden fêtes contribute to a full calendar of varied and interesting events.

The dates of these events obviously vary slightly from year to year and it is as well to check locally before making one of them the focal point or main reason for a holiday at a specific time. Where possible, a guide to dates is given in the gazetteer section but these must not be taken as definite.

Music and the Arts. Cornish village and small town life has its more serious side, of course, and there is a long tradition of good music in the county. Brass bands are taken very seriously indeed, with Camborne and St. Dennis being among the foremost exponents, and the annual Band Contest held at Bugle in June attracts large crowds of knowledgeable supporters.

Male voice and other choirs are also of high standard; Climax (from Camborne), the clay countryside Treviscoe Choir, and Treverva from the west are generally recognised to be among the most effective male choirs. Mixed choirs also come into their own, and during the summer months music festivals of extremely high standard are held in many of Cornwall's parish churches; at St. Endellion, St. Germans, St. Mylor and St. Columb to mention a few at random.

Artists. Ever since artists discovered St. Ives and the unique quality of the light there, the artists' colonies and the tradition of painting have grown and artists are now to be found all over the county. Cornwall's most famous artist was the 18th century portrait painter, **John Opie,** who was born at Harmony Cot, St. Agnes, in May 1761. He painted many well-known society beauties of his day and also produced one now much prized seascape. The late **Peter Lanyon,** is one whose name immediately comes to mind when mentioning artists, whilst **Ben Maile** of Newquay at the present time is achieving considerable success and an enviable reputation on both sides of the Atlantic.

During the summer months many exhibitions of paintings are held and local artists employ a wide variety of techniques to display a great deal of interesting work.

Bernard Leach and **Dame Barbara Hepworth,** both of whom have studios in St. Ives, are undoubtedly the most famous of the contemporary potters and sculptors in Cornwall.

Open Air Theatres. Dramatic art is not forgotten and Cornwall boasts two open air theatres, both of which attract large audiences during the summer months. The unique Minack Theatre occupies a breathtaking position on the cliffside at Porthcurno some 9½ km (6 miles) from Lands End and with the sea as its natural backdrop one can imagine the additional dimension which nature can provide to a performance of Shakespeare's *Tempest*.

Near Perranporth, Piran Round, a medieval theatre in the round, has been revived and for the past few years plays and other forms of entertainment have been produced with considerable success. Some of the plays have been written especially for Piran Round by contemporary Cornish writers whilst others have been modern productions of a cycle of medieval Cornish mystery plays—known as the Ordinalia.

Many towns and villages have arts clubs and dramatic or operatic societies: some of their productions take place during the summer months.

Folk Music. Folk songs and music also have a considerable following and folk clubs throughout the county welcome all who want to sing-along. Folk clubs meet in a variety of unusual and interesting places, ranging from the new Folk Cottage in the Swan Hotel at Truro to the Pipers Folk Club at St. Buryan.

Bell-Ringing. The art or science of bell-ringing has many devotees in Cornwall and visiting ringers are warmly welcomed in most ringing chambers. Method change-ringing is practised in such towers as Truro Cathedral, St. Mary's, Penzance, St. Andrew's, Stratton, and a number of others, mainly in the western half of the county.

Royal Cornwall Show. Cornwall being largely an agricultural county, naturally the Royal Cornwall Agricultural Association's Annual Show, now a three-day event held in the early days of June on a vast permanent site on the A39 between St. Columb and Wadebridge, attracts considerable support from within and without the county. The exhibits in the horse, cattle, sheep and pig classes are regarded as being of very high standard and the flower-show, show-jumping and main-ring attractions provide a first-class day out for the whole family.

The Larger Towns. The impression must not be given, however (or if it has been given then it must not remain), that the Cornish scene only happens in the villages and smaller towns. The handful of larger centres of population such as Truro, the cathedral city and administrative capital of Cornwall, must not be forgotten; nor must the importance of the industrial towns of Camborne and Redruth, the centre of an area now spearheading a resurgence of tin-mining as well as continuing a long engineering tradition, and the economically viable china-clay producing countryside surrounding St. Austell, be overlooked.

Light industry also has its place in such towns as Liskeard, Launceston,

Bodmin, Wadebridge and Helston; and of course Falmouth, with its docks and shipyards, plays a unique part in the county's industrial life.

Fishing, although not so important now as half a century ago, still provides a livelihood for a proportion of the indigenous population and in such places as Padstow, St. Ives, Newlyn, Mevagissey, Fowey and Looe appears to flourish; especially when integrated with trips round the bay and the provision of facilities for holiday-makers to have a day shark- or wreck-fishing.

All this, then, adds up to the Cornwall of today which really does have 'a bit of everything' to attract the visitor. Natural attractions of coast and countryside combine with a nucleus of industrial development to help stabilise the county's economy throughout the year rather than depend entirely on agriculture and tourism. There is also a fresh awareness of the importance of the tourist industry, indicated by the number of commercial and semi-commercial enterprises which provide the visitor with acceptable and interesting alternatives to the beaches and other natural amenities.

The National Trust. The National Trust plays an important part both in these commercial ventures and in the preservation of Cornwall's heritage. Great houses such as Antony or Cotehele, both in East Cornwall, and Lanhydrock just outside Bodmin are splendidly maintained and can be visited. The superb gardens of Trelissick near Truro, Glendurgan near Falmouth and Trengwainton at Penzance are well worth visiting, especially early in the year when the spring flowers and flowering shrubs such as azaleas, camellias and rhododendrons are in full bloom. The 14th century chapel and part of the main castle of St. Michael's Mount, romantically situated on an island (at high water) in Mount's Bay off Marazion, is also owned by the Trust as well as Trerice Manor (near Newquay), the Old Post Office at Tintagel and the East Pool Mine Engine House between Redruth and Camborne.

Further details about these historic places of interest have been incorporated into the appropriate sections of the second part of this book and the National Trust's Information Officer at Saltram House, Plymouth (Plymouth 37579) is always pleased to provide information.

The Romance of Tin-Mining. Most of the towns and villages have their craft shops, local potteries and museums of one sort or another. These are mentioned as places to visit, in other parts of this book. A few of the larger commercial enterprises however are worthy of special mention because they provide much-needed 'wet-weather' venues when the beaches and other outdoor activities are impossible.

Naturally those enterprises reflecting matters which are uniquely Cornish are of special interest, particularly any associated with tin-mining. Mention has already been made of the National Trust's East Pool Mine and museum between Camborne and Redruth, but, by prior arrangement with the Mine Manager concerned, arrangements can also be made to visit two Cornish Mine Engines preserved at mines which are still working. These are at Levant Mine, St. Just (telephone The Manager, Geevor Mine, St. Just (073677) 393), and at South Crofty Mine, Camborne (telephone The Manager, South Crofty, Camborne (02092) 3150).

Cornwall being so rich in mineral ores it was often possible, and more profitable to mine for both tin and copper at the same time. At Dolcoath, near Camborne, for example, much copper was mined from 1720 onwards. It was then discovered that there was also a major tin lode nearby and tin-mining was carried on for the next hundred years. When operations finally ceased after the First World War, the deepest shaft had reached more than 3,000 feet beneath the surface: hence the local saying 'as deep as Dolcoath' used to describe a person who was devious or extra-cunning in business transactions.

Not all mining operations were conducted below ground, however, as tin-streaming was another much-used method of winning tin. An authentic atmosphere of these tin-streaming days has been successfully re-created at Tolgus Tin, just outside Redruth. Here the visitor can watch the whole fascinatingly simple yet effective process in common use more than a century ago, whereby the tin ore is crushed and the tin-oxide separated from the useless gravel, using only water-power.

Historic Monuments. The Department of the Environment maintains a number of historic monuments throughout the county. In the far west of Cornwall the Department looks after the ancient Ballowall Barrow (burial-place) at St. Just, and the ancient villages of Carn Euny near Sancreed and Chysauster outside Penzance. The Chapel of Dupath Well near Callington, **King Doniert's** Stone and Trethevy Quoit at St. Cleer, the Hurlers Stone Circle at Minions and a monolith on the St. Breock Downs near Wadebridge are examples of the diversity of well-preserved monuments cared for by the Department; which also maintains six castles or castle ruins. These are dealt with more fully later in the book.

Museums. Relics of the sea also figure prominently in museums, and specialist collections of nautical miscellanea are also found almost all the way around the coast. Possibly one of the most interesting and unique assortments of such relics has been assembled at Penzance by Mr. Roland Morris in the Maritime Museum attached to the Admiral Benbow Restaurant. For many years Mr. Morris has been involved in deep-sea salvage operations of one sort or another and among his treasures were a cannon, a pewter chamber-pot and a variety of other items recovered a few years ago from the wreck of H.M.S. *Association*, the Flagship of Admiral Sir Cloudesley Shovel, which was lost off the Isles of Scilly when homeward bound after taking Gibraltar.

For those interested in coins the Castle Museum of Coins at Tintagel will provide a diversion.

As has already been mentioned, folklore and superstition played an important part in people's lives in earlier generations. White witches, such as Tamson Blight, well-known in West Cornwall, were common and the ever-present threat of the 'evil-eye' was a curse to be avoided at all costs. Relics of witchcraft linger on and a most impressive and gruesome collection has been assembled at the Museum of Witchcraft at Boscastle. There is also a Museum of Folklore and Witchcraft at Looe.

Disused tin-mine near Truro

A visit to the County Museum at Truro (the Royal Institution of Cornwall), is an absolute must for there can be found relics of every phase of the county's development from the earliest days. Military history is not forgotten at the Regimental Museum of the former Duke of Cornwall's Light Infantry at Bodmin, whilst Cornwall's agrarian past is preserved in several farm museums.

A unique collection of musical automata including various kinds of player pianos, cinema and other organs, can be seen and heard at the Old Mill at St. Keyne, near Liskeard, and for model village devotees those at Polperro, St. Agnes and Lelant provide contrasting styles and interesting comparisons. There is another Museum of Mechanical Music in West Cornwall at Goldsithney (on B3280) not far from Penzance, and a fine collection of horse-drawn carriages at Treskillard, near Camborne.

Of course not all exhibitions in Cornwall are confined to displaying things of the distant past. The Camborne Museum, the Holman Engineering Museum and the School of Mines Museum also at Camborne, whilst obviously tracing the history of mining are situated in the centre of a part of Cornwall that is still industrialised, and are very much of the present.

TRANSPORT

Railways. One of the easiest (though possibly the most expensive) means of travelling to Cornwall is by rail. Regular and fast services, mostly equipped with restaurant or buffet car facilities, direct from Paddington and cross-country from the North of England and the Midlands, converge on Plymouth. The main line then crosses **Brunel's** Royal Albert Bridge and continues right down through the county to Penzance, with stations in the principal towns, Liskeard, St. Austell, Truro, Redruth and Camborne.

Motorail is proving an increasingly popular method of travelling to Cornwall by bringing one's car without having to suffer the trauma of the long and sometimes frustrating journey by road. Regular services from Kensington to St. Austell and Penzance and from Scotland, the North of England and the Midlands to Newton Abbot in Devon, are provided but as timings and facilities offered vary from year to year, intending users of the service would be well advised to enquire at their local travel agents or nearest motorail terminal.

Local trains call at the smaller stations and there are one or two 'rail-heads', for example Bodmin Road, which serve vast areas of the Cornish countryside. Branch lines are rather few in number and although providing effective links with the main line from Looe, Falmouth, Newquay and St. Ives, are of little use as a means of in-county communication.

Bus Services. National Omnibuses provide regular services between most of the larger towns, whilst the rural services linking the smaller communities are less frequent, being basically routes which converge on the larger centres. Private operators fill in as many gaps in the service as possible, but as so many routes are unremunerative, drastic cuts have been made. The visitor is advised to obtain up-to-date local information.

Timetables. Of great benefit to bus users is the fact that, by arrangement with the Cornwall County Council's Transport Committee, the National Omnibus Companies Timetable also includes the timetables of the privately-operated bus services serving some of the more remote, rural areas.

Holiday Routes. Motorists are advised to obtain a copy of the current leaflet issued by the Department of the Environment giving details of the recognised Holiday Routes, which can save many hours of frustration on both outward and return journeys.

These routes are certainly well worth following to avoid delays and traffic queues at such nationally infamous chaos points as the Exeter by-pass or Bodmin or Launceston.

On the journey to Cornwall the A373 and A3072 off the A38 via Tiverton, Crediton, Hatherleigh and Holsworthy avoid hazards met at these places, and the A39 is used to enter Cornwall. This same A39 is also the recommended return route for light traffic; turn off at Stratton on to A3072 after leaving Cornwall then follow the A388 via the North Devon market towns of Torrington, South Molton and Bampton (A361) until the holiday route rejoins the A38 for Taunton. Northbound traffic will be able to join the M5 and London-bound traffic can take the A371 to join the A303 west of Wincanton.

Air Services. Cornwall has no civil airport other than such facilities as are provided by arrangement with the Royal Air Force for Newquay's Civil Air Terminal at St. Mawgan Air Station. British Midland Airways maintain scheduled services from Birmingham, the East Midlands, London (Heathrow) and Manchester whilst Brymon Airways operate an in-county service between Newquay and the Isles of Scilly and Plymouth. British Airways helicopters fly at frequent and regular intervals between the Eastern Green Heliport at Penzance and St. Marys, Isles of Scilly. Advance booking is necessary and at peak periods and week-ends it is advisable to book far in advance to avoid disappointment. (Reservations Office—Penzance 3871).

Ferries and other Boat Links. Until the Tamar Road Bridge was completed in 1961 the only means of road communication between Plymouth and South-East Cornwall was by ferry. The Devonport (Plymouth) to Torpoint (Cornwall) car ferry still provides a regular and frequent service, but as there can be delays, the new bridge is by far the best way of entering the county unless one is travelling to South-East Cornwall.

Car ferries also ply between Fowey and Bodinnick (across the River Fowey) and at King Harry Passage on the River Fal between King Harry and Philleigh to link the Roseland peninsula with Truro and West Cornwall, saving a long drive around Tregony. These services are fairly frequent and regular in summer, but times of evening and Sunday sailings should be checked as these can be sporadic and sometimes non-existent. A regular passenger ferry service links St. Mawes, St. Anthony and Percuil in the Roseland with Falmouth (Prince of Wales Pier) from which there is also a regular passenger service to and from Flushing on the opposite side of Penryn Creek.

The R.M.S. *Scillonian* sails daily in each direction (twice on summer Saturdays) between Penzance and St. Mary's, Isles of Scilly. The crossing, which can be very rough, takes something over three hours depending on weather and tides.

A regular passenger service is provided between Padstow and Rock and other even smaller and more infrequent services operate between Restronguet and Mylor Creeks on the River Fal and Crantock and Newquay (estuary of the River Gannel).

ACTIVITY HOLIDAYS

For the holiday-maker who does not want to merely sit on a beach and laze in the sun, explore moorlands, visit stately homes and great houses or indulge any latent antiquarian interests, Cornwall provides a wide range of activity holidays.

Surfing and Boating. The principal activity holidays are, of course, those associated with the sea and appropriate additional references have been made throughout this guide. Generally speaking, however, on the north coast the Atlantic breakers provide the natural facilities for surf-riding in all its forms, whilst the south coast is best suited to boating of all descriptions in the calmer waters of the English Channel.

Over the past few years Malibu surf-riding has increased enormously, particularly on Cornwall's north coast, where it has been said that the surf at its best rivals that of Australia's famous Bondi Beach.

One of the acknowledged experts in this exciting sport is English and European Champion, Graham Nile, of St. Austell, who is an authority on the subject at his Sports Shop at 7 Duke Street, St. Austell, (telephone St. Austell 2870). Another well-known commercial centre is the Skewjack Surf Centre at Porthcurno (telephone Sennen 287). Cornish-born Gwynedd Haslock, the British Girls Surfing Champion, advises that *all* who attempt to ride the surf must first of all be able to swim really well in the *sea*. Other prerequisites for would-be surfers are to know their own limitations, to try to find a place to experiment where no one else is bathing so that one is sure he or she is not in anybody else's way, to obey the local authority's warnings as to when not to enter the water, and to consult the lifeguards if in any doubt.

The Surf Life Saving Association of Great Britain has two principal centres in Cornwall—at Perranporth and at Bude. Anyone wishing to obtain further information about the sport, in advance of their holiday, is recommended to write to The Administrator, British Surfing Association, Parkstone, Dorset.

Skin-diving, deep-sea shark fishing, bottom fishing, and water-skiing: all these forms of water sport can be carried out on both north and south coasts with most of the larger resorts providing the necessary facilities.

The popularity of canoeing as a holiday activity is increasing, and facilities exist principally in and around the river estuaries. This sport is particularly well-organised at Sennen and in the Penzance area where there is a flourishing Canoe Club (telephone Penzance 4182 for information). The West Cornwall representative of the British Canoe Union can be contacted at Perranporth 3062.

Riding and Pony-Trekking. Inland, of course, horse-riding and pony-trekking are among the principal delights, especially in the moorland areas. Riding establishments are strictly controlled by Act of Parliament and District Councils maintain lists of registered stables and riding schools which are properly conducted within an established code of practice. There are approximately sixty authorised stables in Cornwall, and local information on their whereabouts can easily be obtained.

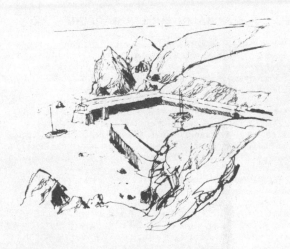

Mullion Cove

Rambling and Climbing. The Cornwall Coast Path and the hundreds of miles of public footpaths provide the various categories of walkers, ramblers and hikers with plenty of opportunities. The Cornwall Ramblers Association (Hon. Sec. Mr. W. J. C. Street, 9 Trelyn, Rock, Wadebridge, telephone Trebetherick 2503) is always pleased to suggest routes and give information. Proper clothing and a good map of sufficient scale to give all the necessary details are essential before embarking on any walking tour.

As there are no really high hills in Cornwall mountaineering or hill-climbing is not really one of the indigenous activities, although the two principal 'heights' of Brown Willy, 419 m (1,375 ft), and Rough Tor, 400 m (1,311 ft), on Bodmin Moor provide some good climbing and the views from other hills such as Helman Tor near Lanivet and Kit Hill near Callington well repay the effort needed to climb them. Toni Carver has compiled and edited a useful book called *Climbing in Cornwall* which contains detailed information about climbs in north, south and east Cornwall. There is also an official publication — *The Climbers Club Guide to Cornwall,* Volumes I and II. Cliff climbing on some of the precipitous rock faces in West Cornwall, particularly around the cliffs of Lands End, is another form of activity, requiring expertise or at least expert guidance and steady nerves. Cliff climbing around Lands End is controlled by the Lands End Climbing Club, and a phone call to Newlyn 3928 will bring information and details of how to join.

CORNISH FOOD AND DRINK

Food. A light-hearted reason why there are so many place names in Cornwall bearing the prefix 'Saint' is that the Devil feared to enter the Duchy lest he was included in the ingredients of a Cornish pasty; his Satanic Majesty having heard that thrifty Cornish housewives were prone to put almost anything they could lay hands on into a pasty.

This is not to be taken as an unfavourable comment on the culinary merits of Cornwall's famous national dish, as the true Cornish pasty, made of best steak with sliced potatoes and other vegetables, e.g. onion or turnip according to taste and crimped into a crisp pastry casing, is a most delicious and satisfying meal. Fish was an acceptable alternative to meat, and apple would be included at one end thus providing both 'mains' and 'afters' in one unit.

Digressing further on the history of the pasty, it is said that this particular form of self-contained meal originated in the mining communities. The pasty's shape was such that it could conveniently be carried in a linen bag in a pocket. It would then be eaten direct from the bag, without a knife and fork, and didn't come into contact with the miners' dirty hands. This method of eating a pasty, that is keeping it whole and starting at one end, is still recognised as being the correct way.

Of course the pasty is not Cornwall's only 'national' dish. Delicacies such as saffron cake and clotted cream are well known, and although marinated pilchards, starry-gazey pies, hogs-puddings, junkets or figgie-'obbin are not quite so well known they are equally delectable. Beware, however, of spurious imitations!

It is regrettable that establishments serving 'national' dishes are few and far between, but from time to time they can occur in the most sophisticated menus. Smoked mackerel is found regularly among the 'starters' and is a very palatable alternative to the more expensive smoked salmon.

Visitors fortunate enough to secure accommodation in farmhouses may well find pasties, saffron cake and fried hogs-pudding on their menus, and supplies of real Cornish cream should be well in evidence. Genuine Cornish cream teas can be obtained almost everywhere—the average price being in the order of 30p—plus, alas, V.A.T.

It would be pointless to list all the inns, restaurants and cafés which offer a wide choice of food at reasonable prices, as nearly all the Cornish towns and villages have these facilities to a greater or lesser extent. Some of the more outstanding and interesting places have been mentioned in the gazetteer or touring section.

Drink. Rough Cider, the drink generally associated with the West Country, can be obtained at most hotels and inns, even though none is actually made in Cornwall. Mead, the 'honeymoon' drink, is made in West Cornwall, and is a potent, sweet concoction.

The St. Austell Brewery and the Devenish Brewery are regarded as the local brewers and own a number of tied houses, but nearly all sell one of the nationally known beers which can be drunk in a variety of surroundings ranging from character inns such as The Finnygook at Crafthole or The Norway at Perranarworthal to the former coaching inns such as The White Hart at Launceston or Tyack's at Camborne and the more sophisticated and modern Drum Major at Bodmin and King Mark at Newquay.

CARAVANNING AND CAMPING

The popularity of caravanning and camping holidays has increased rapidly over the past few years. This fact is nowhere more apparent than in Cornwall, where the narrow roads and lanes simply cannot cope with the volume of traffic at peak periods. Caravan owners need not necessarily be deterred from visiting Cornwall by this fact, as during the early and late season it is easy to tow a caravan around Cornwall, always provided that one's car is of sufficient power to cope with the steep hills which abound in coastal and inland areas alike.

The National Caravan Club has many recommended sites in the county and of course its members are well equipped to bring their caravans into Cornwall and have no difficulty in knowing where to stay. A great many visitors, however, still pile into the county hopefully looking for a good site, and sometimes without any idea of what they really want. Sometimes caravanners are forced to spend the night, or even several nights, on lay-bys beside main roads.

There are many excellent caravan and camping sites in Cornwall equipped with all the facilities needed to complete one's holiday enjoyment. The larger sites have shops, modern toilet blocks with launderettes and drying rooms, bars, restaurants and entertainments of one sort or another. Naturally such sites are well patronised and early booking is a necessity. The Cornwall Caravan and Chalet Park Owners Association have more than fifty recommended sites not only in or near the popular coastal resorts, but also in some delightful rural areas. A list of the sites whose owners are members of the Association can be obtained from the Hon. Secretary at Maen Valley Caravan Park, Falmouth, and the Cornwall Tourist Board can also assist in finding caravan and camping sites.

GENERAL INFORMATION

Cornwall Tourist Board. Tourism is big business in Cornwall and it is refreshing and not really surprising to find that this very independent and individualistic county has its own Tourist Board. The Cornwall Tourist Board publishes a register of approved accommodation in all price ranges and categories. Roadside information bureaux are open during the season to assist tourists in finding accommodation if they arrive without already having made bookings, and a useful advance booking service is also available through the Board's Central Office at County Hall, Truro (Truro 4282) from which address other information, can be obtained.

Local Newspapers. The only daily newspaper serving Cornwall is the Plymouth-based *Western Morning News* which, with the complementary *Western Evening Herald,* provides ample coverage of international, national and local topics. Nine local newspapers are published weekly and it is to these that the visitor is recommended to refer for advertisements of forthcoming events and amusements, entertainments and places where one can eat and drink.

The northern part of the county is served by the *Cornish and Devon Post* published in Launceston each Saturday, while the south-east relies on the *Cornish Times* published on Fridays at Liskeard. The whole of mid-Cornwall is covered by the various editions of one of the largest weeklies, the *Cornish Guardian* published on Thursday at Bodmin. The *West Briton* is published on Thursday at Truro, and Camborne, Redruth, Falmouth and Helston areas have their own paper known as the *'Packet'* series: the *Camborne Redruth Packet* is published on Wednesdays and the other two on Friday. The far west and the Isles of Scilly use *The Cornishman* published on Thursday at Penzance and more locally, the *St. Ives Times* and *Echo* published at St. Ives on Friday. The local Sunday newspaper is *The Independent* published in Plymouth.

HOLIDAY AREAS AND TOURING ROUTES

Although on 1st April, 1974, in common with the rest of the country, the major reorganisation of local government affected Cornwall with the result that it now comprises six administrative districts, for purposes of this guide-book it is felt that it would be expedient to divide the county into four areas only.

The elongated shape of the Cornish peninsula is split north and south by the main A30 trunk road which lends itself to an easily definable boundary, and the estuary of the River Gannel at Newquay on the north coast and the great promontory of the Dodman on the south coast, provide natural divisions east and west to separate the county into the four areas.

The first of these will be identified as North Cornwall, and although it covers the whole of the new county district of North Cornwall, it also includes other holiday areas in the northern part of Restormel District. East Cornwall is basically the new District of Caradon plus some areas from the southern part of Restormel District. West Cornwall will include the whole of the District of Penwith, together with the northern areas of the Carrick and Kerrier Districts, whereas South Cornwall will be the southern parts of those Districts.

The coastal holiday centres have been described in geographical order towards Lands End. The inland touring centres have been similarly dealt with and grouped according to the appropriate trunk road A39, A30 or A38.

Throughout the descriptions of recommended tours in this section, places suggested as holiday or touring centres have been printed thus **Newquay** to permit easy cross-reference between recommended routes. Places described in the gazetteer section have been printed thus *St. Mawgan-in-Pydar.*

NORTH CORNWALL

This division of the county is the largest in area, extending from the most northerly parish of *Morwenstow,* southwards to where the A30 trunk road enters the county over Polson Bridge just east of **Launceston.** The A30 then becomes the boundary of this North Cornwall area as far west as its junction with the A39 at Fraddon, then there must be an arbitrary boundary northwards to meet the estuary of the River Gannel at **Newquay.**

There are two outstanding features of this northernmost part of Cornwall; the splendid Atlantic coast and the wonderful uplands of Bodmin Moor. The principal holiday centres are **Bude, Tintagel,** Polzeath, **Padstow,** and of course, the important resort of Newquay. There are, however, five inland towns, **Camelford, Wadebridge** and **St. Columb** on the A39 and Launceston and **Bodmin** farther inland on the A30, all ideally situated as touring centres for those who prefer to make daily trips to the coast and also want to visit and explore the surrounding countryside. The popular holiday centre of Bude, or really Bude Haven, is the starting place for what will in effect be a detailed journey through Cornwall.

BUDE

As it stands today **Bude** is really a new town grafted on to the ancient market town of *Stratton* about 2 km (1½ miles) inland. The area explored from Bude ranges from *Morwenstow* in the north across the whole extent of Bude Bay, Widemouth Bay and Crackington Haven right down to *Boscastle*.

In many guide books and by many coach tour operators Bude is also linked with the lovely little north Devon village of Clovelly. Because of its steep cobbled streets Clovelly is unique, and it would be altogether wrong in a guide book such as this not to mention the lovely areas of North Devon which can be reached from Bude after an hour or so car's journey.

Bude has magnificent bathing and surfing beaches and although caution must always be used when entering the water at unsafe states of the tide, great fun can nevertheless be had with a surfboard. Crooklets and Summerleaze beaches, or Widemouth Bay itself are magnificent stretches of sand.

As one would expect of a modern seaside resort, Bude has most of the amenities including a free swimming pool right on the beach, and a golf course. When tired of the sea one can always explore the ancient town of *Stratton* with its quaint streets and old inns. Farther afield are the moors and the upper reaches of the River Tamar, Cornwall's natural boundary with the neighbouring county of Devon. The 12th-century Ebbingford Manor in Vicarage Road is also an extremely interesting building but at the present time, like Penfound Manor a few miles away, is not generally open to the public. In the immediate vicinity of Bude there is also the charming little village of Poughill where the church, dedicated to St. Olaf, has a fine wagon roof and 16th-century bench ends.

TINTAGEL

Tintagel with its castle and stories of King Arthur, must surely be one of the best known places in Cornwall if not in the whole of the West Country. Tintagel Head rises from 'The Island', which is not really an island but a spur of rocky cliffs connected to the mainland. In 1140 Reginald, Earl of Cornwall, started building what is now known as King Arthur's Castle. A century or so afterwards a later Earl of Cornwall added more buildings on the mainland, joined to the island by a bridge.

After the Civil War however, Tintagel Castle fell into disuse and is now merely a romantic ruin conjuring up visions of King Arthur, of Merlin the magician, of Queen Guinevere, Sir Galahad, Sir Lancelot and all the other legendary Knights of the Round Table. These interesting ruins are now in the custody of the Department of the Environment and are well worth a visit for their historical value, quite apart from any Arthurian associations. The castle ruins are open throughout the year during the hours of daylight.

One must not think however, that all Tintagel's attractions are centred round this clifftop fortress. There is an ancient parish church standing in a very exposed position, where even the tombstones must be buttressed against the force of the Atlantic gales. To the west of the island there are remains of what was almost certainly a 4th century Celtic monastery.

Modern Tintagel is something of an anti-climax, catering as it does for holiday makers en masse, and in particular for coach parties who make almost an American-style, whistle-stop pilgrimage to King Arthur's Castle. In the main street however, the Old Post Office, once a 14th-century manorhouse, is an authentic relic of the past. Now the property of the National Trust, this building is open to the public between April and mid-October during normal hours.

At King Arthur's Hall in Fore Street a fifty year old vision of the 20th-century age of chivalry can be seen. To some this hall may seem spurious and unworthy, but to others it no doubt has a certain interest in its own right in that it represents an attempt to re-create something of the atmosphere that could have surrounded King Arthur's court.

There is considerable controversy concerning the various versions of the Arthurian legend. Rather it is something which has been handed down by oral tradition thus forming part of the folklore of this part of Cornwall. The mere fact that proof of historical authenticity is lacking need not deter the visitor from enjoying the atmosphere of Tintagel Castle and all that goes with the local versions of one of the best known of all legends.

Tintagel is of course a very good holiday centre. To the north there is **Bude** and *Boscastle* and to the south Trebarwith Strand, a wide expanse of sand, which, particularly at low tide, is ideal for sea bathing and sun-bathing. There are also a number of rocky pools where children may safely play. Tregardock and Strangles Beaches to the south of Trebarwith are typical of the many secluded little coves which are to be found in this attractive part of North Cornwall.

POLZEATH and the Camel Coast

The magnificent stretch of Atlantic coastline from the Devon border to the estuary of the River Camel divides easily into three holiday areas each with its own centre. Mention has already been made of **Bude** and **Tintagel** and the third area to the north of the Camel River is regarded by many as being the most attractive of all holiday areas. The little village of *St. Endellion* lies at the heart of this particular area which stretches from Port Isaac Bay through Port Gaverne, Port Quin and *Port Isaac* itself, right around Pentire Head to **Polzeath,** Trebetherick and *Rock*. The gazetteer will contain references to these places and although the resident village population of Polzeath is less than five hundred it nevertheless provides a very good centre from which to explore this fascinating area.

The Pentire peninsula is National Trust property and a walk to Rumps

Point to the north east is well worth while for the view of the cliffs. On the other side of Pentire Point lies Hayle Bay, not to be confused with the seaport of Hayle and its estuary in the west of the county. There are superb sandy beaches at Pentireglaze and Polzeath, and a mile or two farther on is the village of Trebetherick, which has some good hotels.

The picturesque golf links of St. Enodoc overlook Daymer Bay and the River Camel. Here is the little Norman church of St. Enodoc, beloved of **Sir John Betjeman,** the Poet Laureate, as it was in this area of Cornwall he spent his childhood. There is a memorial to Sir John's father in the church which for centuries was buried under the sands, but has been restored and from its unique situation alone is well worth a visit.

The sandy foreshore of *Rock* is becoming increasingly popular as a centre for sailing and other forms of water-sports including water-skiing.

PADSTOW

Across the river from *Rock* and **Polzeath** lies **Padstow,** or Petrocstow. This most picturesque town, is a warren of narrow streets converging on the harbour with its fishing boats and yachts and dinghies. A passenger service runs frequently to Rock across the Camel estuary. From North Quay a footpath follows the riverbank to St. George's Well, a little bay so named because there is a local tradition that England's Patron Saint landed there. The path then continues as far as Harbour Cove where one can swim or sunbathe on the soft sand. Towards the open sea Pentire Head and Stepper Point guard the entrance to the estuary and harbour. The Doombar, a great sand bank on which many fine ships have been wrecked, stretches across the river, and the very narrow channel calls for considerable navigational skill to enable ships to pass safely at low tide.

In recent years Padstow has become nationally known throughout the 'folk' world, for its celebration of the coming of summer on May 1st. This publicity is not always kindly received by the Padstonians, who, quite rightly, feel that an unruly 'outside' element tends to spoil May Day for them, and for those who for many years have flocked there from the surrounding countryside. The proceedings begin just after midnight, and then after a few hours rest, a crowd of musicians, singers and dancers accompany the fearsome high-stepping 'Obby 'Oss on its several tours of the town from dawn until dusk. Led by the 'Teaser' brandishing a gaily decorated club, the 'Obby 'Oss and its attendant ceremonies are regarded as the survival of an ancient fertility rite. An extremely authoritative book on the history of the celebrations and the meaning behind them has been written by Donald Rawe, a Padstonian, and Bard of the Cornish Gorsedd.

The many excellent beaches within easy reach of Padstow underline its value as a holiday centre. From nearby Trevone Bay one can follow an interesting section of the Cornwall Coast Path along the clifftop by Tregudda towards Daymer Beacon and on the other side it is a comparatively easy walk to Harlyn Bay. From Mother Ivey's Bay there is a toll road to the lighthouse at *Trevose Head* where on a fine day Hartland

Padstow 'Obby 'Oss Dance

Point in Devon to the north east and Godrevy Point near St. Ives to the west are visible. Constantine Bay, Booby's Bay, Treyarnon Bay and Porthcothan Bay are all good bathing and surfing beaches, providing reasonable care is taken. Readily accessible car parks, beachside shops and public conveniences are provided.

Padstow possesses an interesting church, an excellent small museum, very local in its origin, housed in the Institute building in the middle of the town and in Fentonluna Lane there is a tropical zoological bird garden, open all the year round, which provides hours of fascination for adults and children alike.

At Dennis Cove, a holiday complex provides excellent facilities for riding, boating and a putting course, and there is also a swimming pool.

The Elizabethan manor house of Prideaux Place overlooks the town from the reputed site of St. Petroc's monastery. Here there is a deer park and the house is reputed to be haunted by two ghosts. Beside the North Quay is the 15th century Abbey House, originally a religious residence,

and on South Quay is the old Courthouse. To the seaward a public open
space known as St. Saviour's Field provides a wonderful vantage point
from which to see the comings and goings of the busy little harbour.

NEWQUAY

Newquay is probably the best known of all the Cornish holiday resorts and
deservedly so. It is here that all that Cornwall's north coast has to offer
seems to converge, with the splendid beaches which almost defy description,
and for which Newquay has become internationally famous.

Thousands of visitors flock to Newquay every year to laze on the soft
sand, ride the Atlantic surf and enjoy the amenities provided. Before
becoming completely submerged by the facilities offered by the resort, it is
worthwhile digressing briefly on the history of Newquay and its surrounding hinterland.

To the vast majority of people who only know Newquay for a fortnight
or so in the middle of a 20th century summer, it may come as a surprise to
learn that some sixteen hundred years ago there was a settlement on
Porth Island. Here ore from Whipsiderry was smelted to make weapons
for the natives to defend themselves from the savage tribes who inhabited
the mainland.

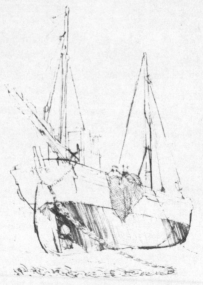

Fishing-boat

Details of the life led by these early inhabitants of Porth Island came to light in 1939 when their burial kists were excavated. The chieftains were buried in dome-shaped barrows on the surrounding clifftops. Traces of these barrows are still visible today on the Barrowfields, the open space in front of the modern hotels which overlook Narrowcliff and Newquay's beaches.

A thousand years later in the late 18th century, Newquay's fishing industry became established. The old fish lofts and fish cellars in and around Fore Street were evidence of this, but nowadays only the Huer's House on the headland remains as a tangible reminder of those days. From there the 'huer' or caller kept watch for the shoals of pilchards. On sighting them he would shout 'Heva' (from the Cornish 'Hevsa'—a shoal of fish) and the fishermen waiting below in the harbour would then put to sea and catch the fish.

In 1874 Squire Treffry opened a mineral railway line from Par through the Luxulyan Valley and down across the Goss Moor to Newquay. There was also a small ship-building industry. Among the boats locally built were the renowned Newquay Pilot Gigs. When a trading vessel appeared off-shore the pilot gigs would set out towards her. The first crew to reach her got the job of piloting her into harbour and working her cargo. Naturally there was great rivalry between the crews. Six gigs still survive: there are three in Newquay harbour, and the other three have been loaned to the Isles of Scilly.

Smuggling also had its part in the history of old Newquay. The seemingly never-ending contest between the smugglers and the revenue men has been the source of many stories. Every kind of contraband was successfully smuggled by well organised crews. Crantock men were supposed to be the most daring and are reputed to have used the Albion Inn and the belfry of the parish church as both rendezvous and stores. Many cargoes were run into the honeycomb of caves under the headlands and stored in places like the aptly-named Tea Caverns under the Huer's House.

In defence of these smugglers, though, it must be said that they did not indulge in wrecking. Cornishmen have long been wrongly maligned for the practice of showing false lights to entice ships to alter their course, founder on the rocks and thus fall prey to the waiting marauders.

By the 1920s fishing had declined, but the summer visitors arrived in increasing numbers and Newquay's prosperity was assured. After the Second World War Newquay's share of the holiday trade increased rapidly until nowadays probably some 80,000 visitors come to this area each year.

In the warm Trenance valley there is a most attractive boating lake and gardens, a bowling green (one of many in Newquay), a series of tennis courts and a Zoo—so much in fact that an entire day can be spent enjoying this particular part of the town alone. Riding schools, pitch and putt courses, pony-trekking, surf-riding, caravan and camping facilities all contribute to the holiday pattern of Newquay. There is good indoor entertainment at the Cosy Nook Theatre and Newquay Theatre, with dancing in most of the larger hotel ballrooms and at the Blue Lagoon, making Newquay one of the few resorts where it is still possible to enjoy a complete holiday without having to use a car.

Facilities exist for air-travel from several parts of the British Isles to the Newquay Civil Air Terminal at St. Mawgan R.A.F. Station.

The branch railway line from Par is still open to Newquay and there are connections with all the principal trains from London and other parts of Britain. Coach operators also maintain regular 7-day and 14-day package tours to Cornwall using Newquay as a principal stopping-place.

CAMELFORD

Camelford is a compact little town with a population of just over a thousand, and has been chosen as a touring centre not because it has overmuch accommodation, but rather as a topographical choice. It has the undoubted advantage of being on the main A39 trunk road and from it very good roads fan out towards coast and country in just about every direction. Good accommodation can, however, be found in excellent smaller bed and breakfast or guest house establishments in the vicinity.

Camelford has a long history and is linked with the Cornish Arthurian legends as it is regarded as Camelot. In A.D. 823 the great battle of Slaughterbridge took place between the Britons and the Saxons but no-one really knows whether it was this battle that caused the death of King Arthur.

Camelford has been a market town since the 13th century, but remains to this day a rather quiet little country town—a starting place for exploration of the principal heights of Bodmin Moor. Rough Tor rises to 400 m (1,311 ft) and has the 43rd Wessex Division War Memorial on its summit, and Brown Willy, a little farther away, rises to 419 m (1,375 ft). There are also two rather splendid earth works at Castle Gough and Helstone Round. The area known as Crowdy Marsh has many varieties of birds and other wild life and there are also burial grounds probably some three thousand years old.

The moors are the most outstanding feature of this part of inland Cornwall. From Davidstow in the north to *St. Neot* and *St. Cleer* in the south it is a little over 25 km (13 miles) and from South Petherwin and North Hill in the east to *St. Breward* and *Blisland* in the west it is almost the same distance, making Bodmin Moor's total area cover about 440 sq km (170 sq miles). Stone Age relics, probably dating from 3,000 BC are to be found near St. Breward Church, near Rough Tor, near the De Lank River and at Garrow Tor. Bronze Age relics, dating from 2,000 BC also exist on that part of Garrow Downs known as King Arthur's Hall. Celtic Iron Age relics, such as the hut circle between Rough Tor and Brown Willy are reputed to have some association with the ubiquitous St. Petroc. Most of the rivers of Central Cornwall rise here on the moor, the two most notable being the Fowey and the Camel. The rather less grand

De Lank River must not however be underestimated as it supplies a considerable amount of its basic ingredient to the Water Authority. The Rivers Allen and Valency also rise on the moors and flow through their own beautiful wooded valleys. The Allen joins the Camel just outside Wadebridge and the Valency flows into the Atlantic at *Boscastle*. The Rivers Inny and Lynher also rise here on the moor.

Camelford thus provides an ideal centre from which to explore the moorlands and uplands of old Cornwall, and two car tours out on to the moors are included at Routes 1 and 5. The other routes from Camelford visit **Bude** and the extreme north of the county and **Tintagel** and King Arthur's Country.

Route 1   Bodmin Moor   (Route A)

From **Camelford** take A39 for nearly 5 km (3 miles), turning off on to A395. This will take you through Davidstow and Hallworthy and across Wilsey Down, which gives fine views of Bodmin Moor. Some 3½ km (2 miles) after Hallworthy, near Cold Northcott, turn right towards the little village of St. Clether, which has a well-preserved Holy Well Chapel near the parish church. From St. Clether go back to the minor road, turn right and follow sign-posts to Laneast and thence down to the village of *Altarnun*.

From Altarnun travel south to join A30 at Five Lanes, turn right and follow the trunk road through Trewint and past Jamaica Inn over Bodmin Moor as far as Cardinham Cross. Here turn right, following the signs to *Blisland* and thence across the moors again to either *St. Breward*, passing the granite quarries of Hantergantic, or join the B3266 for *St. Tudy* to rejoin the A39 near Kelly Green to return via the wooded Allen Valley to Camelford.

Route 2   King Arthur's Country and the Camel Coast

Take A39 northward, past Davidstow and over Titchbarrow, where superb views across Bodmin Moor and far away Dartmoor and, to the seaward, Lundy Island, can be seen, as far as Tresparrett Posts, about 11 km (7 miles). Turn left and join B3263 for *Boscastle*. The road continues through Trevalga and the beautiful Rocky Valley with St. Nectan's Kieve, giving magnificent views of the north Cornish coast. After negotiating Bossiney Hill, the tourist arrives at **Tintagel.**

The road then goes south and west towards Trebarwith Strand and Tregardock Beach, or else inland through the slate countryside around *Delabole* (B3314). Still going westward the tourist may either continue on B3314 past the collegiate church of *St. Endellion,* with perhaps a stop for refreshment at the Cornish Arms at Pendoggett, or fork right (sign-posted Port Isaac) and so out again towards the cliffs. This latter route would take in the National Trust Village of Port Gaverne, picturesque *Port Isaac* and finally Port Quin, Pentireglaze and Polzeath. From Polzeath a pretty road follows the northern bank of the Camel Estuary past Trebetherick, Daymer Bay and St. Enodoc to the vast expanse of sand at *Rock*.

The return route can be either via the pretty little inland villages of St. Minver and *St. Kew* to re-join the A39 at St. Kew Highway or via a narrow country road through Stoptide, Porthilly, Trevelver and Dinham to re-join B3314 and cross over Trewornan Bridge, joining A39 at the traffic lights east of **Wadebridge.** In either case follow A39 back to **Camelford.**

Route 3   Bude and the North

From Camelford follow A39 to the county boundary, visiting en route the ancient town of *Stratton,* and the villages of *Kilkhampton* and *Morwenstow.* The return journey will take much longer and will include some of the most impressive coastal scenery in Cornwall.

From Kilkhampton follow the coast road through the Coombe Valley and Duckpool to arrive in Bude via Poughill and Stamford Hill, the scene of the bloody battle between Sir Bevil Grenville's Cavaliers and the Roundheads during the Civil War.

From **Bude** the coast road passes the wonderful beach at Widemouth and then continues to the delightful little sea-girt village of Crackington Haven. Keeping along the smaller coast roads one reaches Beeney Cliff and the sequestered village of St. Juliot in the valley of the Valency. Both Rusey beach and Beeney Cliffs have associations with Thomas Hardy, the novelist, and the church for which he prepared restoration plans contains memorials to him. Return to Camelford via B3266.

Route 5   Bodmin Moor   (Route B)
From **Camelford** take A395 to and from **Launceston** and follow Route 5 (Launceston).

WADEBRIDGE
This pleasant market town is suggested as a touring centre for precisely the same reasons as are the towns of **St. Columb** and **Camelford.** These three towns, which straddle and are linked by the A39 trunk road, are sufficiently inland to attract many visitors who do not wish to spend their entire holiday at the seaside.

Wadebridge's principal glory is Parson Loveybond's 15th-century bridge of 17 arches. This has been carefully renovated in recent years by Cornwall's Highways Department and widened slightly in an attempt to make Wadebridge less of a problem to the motorist. On arrival in Wadebridge one cannot fail to notice its lack of a parish church in the centre of the town. According to Sir John Betjeman the fact that the parish churches of Egloshayle and St. Breock are both well away from the main centre of population indicates that this is a settlement of Medieval, and not Celtic, origin.

Egloshayle, on the A389 road leading to **Bodmin,** is mainly a row of cottages and houses along the river bank. The very fine recreation ground has one of Cornwall's few county cricket grounds. St. Breock, on the other hand, is a remote rural village situated in a delightfully wooded valley.

Wadebridge is an excellent centre for exploring the north coast and the interesting villages surrounding Bodmin Moor such as St. Mabyn, *St. Tudy, Blisland* and *St. Breward* which are within easy reach of each other and can all be visited in the course of half a day. **Padstow** is only a short distance away by a pleasant road leading through the attractive little villages of Little Petherick and St. Issey. St. Issey is well known locally for The Ring o' Bells, an inn which boasts good accommodation and food. There are in fact many inns in Cornwall under the sign of The Ring o' Bells and they are all well within sight and sound of a church tower.

It was a matter of local pride in Wadebridge that it was the first place in Cornwall to have a railway. As far back as 1834 a line ran to Wenford Bridge near *St. Breward* and was used to convey granite from the Hantergantic Quarry on the moor. Alas, the branch to Bodmin and Padstow, in common with a number of other picturesque branch lines throughout the country, was axed when the railway services were drastically reduced some years ago. At the present time, however proposals to re-open the delightful Wadebridge-Padstow section as a narrow-gauge 'Bluebell' line are being seriously considered.

Four suggested road-routes can easily be followed from Wadebridge which together take in all that is best in this northern part of Cornwall.

Church of St. Mawgan-in-Pydar

Route 1 Bodmin Moor (Route A)
Take A39 to *Camelford* via Allen Valley then follow Route 1. Return on A39 after visiting *St. Tudy*.

Route 2 King Arthur's Country and the Camel Coast
Take A39 to Tresparrett Posts, via **Camelford,** then follow Route 2 (Camelford) which finishes at **Wadebridge.**

Route 3 Bude and The North
From **Wadebridge** take the A39 northwards over open country dominated on the right by the tall tower of St. Mabyn Church and on the left by the valley which includes such attractive villages as Chapel Amble with the old-world Maltsters Arms, and *St. Kew* with its lovely church. At St. Kew Highway on the A39 itself there is a Tropical Bird Garden, after which one enters the beautiful Allen Valley, resplendent in autumn with leaves of every imaginable shade, and in spring picturesque with bluebells and primroses and the fresh green of the trees. At Knights Mill turn right and go on to **Camelford.**

A diversion to the left leads to Lanteglos, a charming little church town in a wooded valley, which boasts Lanteglos Farmhouse Hotel—well worth visiting for a good place to stay or for a meal. At Advent there is a delightful little church in a field, completely cut off from any apparent centre of population.

From Camelford follow Route 3 (Camelford), later returning to Wadebridge from Camelford on A39.

Route 9   Padstow and the North Coast

Take the A39 westwards past the permanent showground of the Royal Cornwall Agricultural Association to Hal's Grave and fork right on A389 for **Padstow.** After visiting Padstow and *Trevose Head* take B3276 (coast road) via Harlyn, Treyarnon and Porthcothan Bays, past Bedruthan Steps to Trenance, Mawgan Porth, Watergate Bay, Porth and **Newquay.**

Return either via A3059 to **St. Columb Major,** thence A39 to **Wadebridge,** or from Trevarrian take the minor road to *St. Mawgan-in-Pydar,* thence to St. Columb Major via Carnanton Woods.

ST. COLUMB MAJOR

St. Columb has been chosen as a touring centre because of its situation on the A39, and holiday accommodation is varied and reasonably-priced. No less than 21 beaches are within a half hour car ride and the town itself provides sufficient facilities and interests to complete a good holiday.

In 1333 **Edward III** granted a market charter to **St. Columb** in recognition of services rendered by the Lord of the Manor, Sir John Arundell, at the Battle of Halidon Hill. The fact that St. Columb is a chartered market town is of considerable pride to the inhabitants who are most offended if anyone calls it a village.

At Shrovetide, Townsmen and Countrymen do battle for possession of the silver ball. The origin of the game of hurling is lost in antiquity although it may be the survival of yet another fertility rite. The rising of the silver ball high in the air as it is thrown between the contending parties is also thought to signify the coming of spring, by symbolising the time when the noonday sun daily rises higher in the heavens. The author of this present guide who is a Bard of the Cornish Gorsedd has also written a book on the history and traditions of Cornwall's ancient national sport.

The Red Lion Hotel was once a coaching inn. A former landlord, James Polkinghorne, was a celebrated Cornish heavyweight wrestler who wrestled a mighty encounter with Abraham Cann of Devon.

The parish church of St. Columba is one of the finest in Cornwall and contains interesting modern woodwork in addition to a number of medieval bench-ends. The Longstone in the churchyard of the little church of St. Francis at Indian Queens was thought by Charles Henderson to be the tombstone of a Roman soldier, whilst on St. Breock Downs between **Wadebridge** and St. Columb is a stone row, the Nine Maidens, reputed to be girls petrified for dancing on the Sabbath.

Because St. Columb is so centrally situated in northern mid-Cornwall, it provides an ideal starting point for nearly all the suggested routes, details of which follow.

Route 1   Bodmin Moor   (Route A)
Take A39 over St. Breock Downs, passing the Nine Maidens (which can
be visited on foot) to **Camelford.** Admire the magnificent panoramic view
of the Camel Estuary and surrounding countryside from St. Eval to St.
Issey, Trebetherick, *St. Endellion* and the distant Bodmin Moor with
Rough Tor and Brown Willy clearly visible. Then follow Route 1
(Camelford) returning to **St. Columb Major** also on A39.

Route 2   King Arthur's Country and the Camel Coast
Take A39 through **Wadebridge** and **Camelford** to Tresparrett Posts and
thence as Route 2 (Camelford).
   Return from Wadebridge on A39.

Route 3   Bude and The North
Join this route at, and return from **Camelford** using A39 via **Wadebridge.**

Route 5   Bodmin Moor   (Route B)
Take A39 to **Wadebridge** and **Camelford** then A395 over Wilsey Down to
Launceston. Then follow Route 5 (Launceston). Return from Jamaica Inn,
Bolventor via A30 through **Bodmin** to Goss Moor, turning off at Castle-an-
Dinas on the Class III road for **St. Columb.**

Route 6   The Tamar Valley   (and Plymouth)
Route 7   The Rame Peninsula and Mount Edgcumbe Country Park
Joint these routes at, and return from, **Liskeard** using A30 to **Bodmin** and
A38 (Glynn Valley Road) to Liskeard.

Route 9   Padstow and the North Coast
Take A39 to Winnards Perch and turn left on to B3274 for **Padstow.**
Follow Route 9 **(Wadebridge)** to return to **Newquay** and **St. Columb Major.**

Route 10   Lanhydrock House, Looe and the Fowey Estuary
Take the Class III road to join A30 at Goss Moor, turn left and join
Route 10 **(St. Austell)** at Reperry Fork.
   Return from St. Austell via A391 to Stenalees, thence B3274 to *Roche.*
Join A30 at Roche Cross and the Class III road at Castle-an-Dinas for
St. Columb.

Route 14   The China-Clay Countryside and the Camel Valley
From **St. Columb** take A39 to Indian Queens (in the same parish) join the
A30 then take the B3278 to St. Dennis, Nanpean and Whitemoor, thence
through Little America over Longstone Downs, 296 m (971 ft), and on
to Hensbarrow Downs, 313 m (1,026 ft). From these vantage points
almost the whole of mid-Cornwall (Restormel District) can be seen and a
good view obtained of the extent of the china-clay operations. Follow
signposts to Bugle and thence via minor roads to Tremodrett to join
A30 at Victoria. Turn right and then left fork for West Downs. The
wooded upper reaches of the River Camel can now be driven through
on a whole series of minor roads following the principal signposts to
Wadebridge via Tremore, Ruthern Bridge, Grogley, Hustyn and Burlawn.
   Return to St. Columb either via Wadebridge on A39 or using the
pleasant country roads over St. Breock Downs through Rosenannon and
St. Wenn.

Route 15   The Roseland Peninsula and Truro
From **St. Columb** take A39 to Fraddon to join A30 for a short distance
westwards. At Blue Anchor fork left (signed Grampound Road) to
Scarcewater Cross and turn left on to A3058 for *St. Stephen-in-Brannel*.
Fork right on to minor road for Sticker to cross A390, thence to London
Apprentice on B3273 for Pentewan and **Mevagissey.** Follow coast road
through Portmellon to Gorran (Gorran Haven), Caerhayes (Castle and
Porthluney beach), Portloe and *Veryan*.

From Veryan join A3078 for **St. Mawes** with diversions for Portscatho,
St. Anthony-in-Roseland (Place Manor) and Gerrans as required.

Return from *St. Mawes* to *St. Just-in-Roseland* and, via King Harry
Ferry to join A39 at Playing Place and return to St. Columb via **Truro,**
Tresillian and Ladock.

Route 16   Newquay, Perranporth, the North Cliffs and the Mining Division
Take the A3059 to **Newquay,** skirting the important Royal Air Force
Station, St Mawgan. Leave Newquay by the A3075 for Goonhavern and
Perranporth and then follow directions for Route 16 (Truro).

Return from **Truro** by A39 (Ladock Valley).

Route 17   Falmouth and the Helford River
This route can be joined by taking A39 to and from **Truro.**

Route 18   Helston and the Lizard Peninsula

Route 19   The West Coast

Lands End

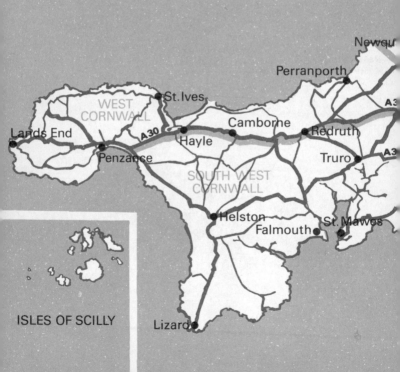

Cornwall and the Isles of Scilly

Newqu

Perranporth

St.Ives

WEST CORNWALL

A30

A3

Camborne

Lands End

Hayle

Redruth

A3

Penzance

Truro

SOUTH WEST CORNWALL

Helston

St. Mawes

Falmouth

ISLES OF SCILLY

Lizard

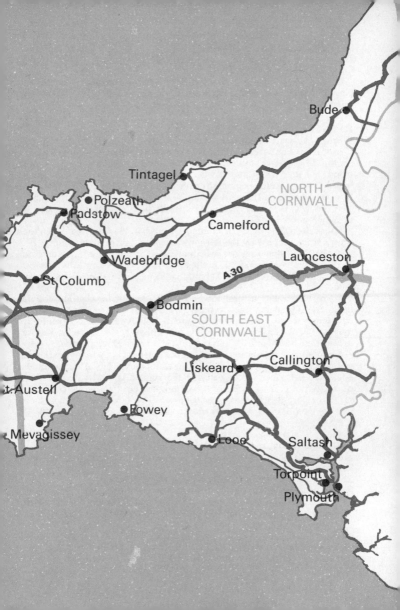

Route 20   Lands End Peninsula
These routes can be joined by taking A39 through **Truro** to Treluswell Cross and thence A394 to **Helston.**

Return either on the same route or on A30 from **Penzance** or *Marazion,* through **Hayle, Camborne, Redruth** to Fraddon and then A39 to **St. Columb.**

LAUNCESTON

Formerly known as Dunheved, **Launceston** is regarded as the 'Gateway to Cornwall' as one enters from Devon over Polson Bridge on the A30.

Until 1835 Launceston was the county town, it was also the assize town from 1177 until 1838. Its recorded history goes back more than eleven hundred years. At the beginning of the 10th century it had the only Royal Mint in the county. Its castle was built in A.D. 1080 by Robert, Count of Mortain and the first Earl of Cornwall, half-brother to William the Conqueror.

Launceston Castle played an important part in the Civil War when for a time it was occupied by the Parliamentarians, and in 1656 George Fox, the founder of the Quakers, was imprisoned in its dungeon. Launceston has some splendid Georgian houses and in the town centre is the 16th-century parish church of St. Mary Magdalene with its beautifully carved granite exterior.

Primarily an agricultural town, Launceston also has good shopping facilities, open spaces like Coronation Park and ample opportunities for golf, tennis, bowls, fishing and swimming. An extremely good centre for touring Cornwall, it has the added advantage of its situation midway between the north and south coasts just inside the Devon border.

Holiday accommodation in the Launceston area is abundant and good, and at Lewdown on the A30 a Cornwall Tourist Board Accommodation Bureau is open all day during the summer months to help those who have not previously booked accommodation. From Launceston it is easy to explore **Bodmin Moor** and the lovely Tamar Valley and these therefore are the principal routes which the visitor is recommended to follow.

Route 1   Bodmin Moor   (Route A)
From **Launceston** travel westwards on A30 as far as Five Lanes, from where the tourist can follow Route 1 **(Camelford)** taking the instructions in the second paragraph first.

Route 2   King Arthur's Country and the Camel Coast
From **Launceston** take A30 to Kennards House, then A395 to Hallworthy and B3262 to join A39. Turn right and follow Route 2 **(Camelford)** eventually returning from Camelford to Launceston as in Route 4 (A39, A395, and A30).

Route 4   Bude
From **Launceston** drive due north on B3254 through Yeolmbridge. After about 17 km (11 miles), to the left is the little village of *Week St. Mary* and

its almost legendary associations with Dame Thomasina Perceval a local girl who became the wife of a Lord Mayor of London but never forgot her native village.

The main road leads directly to **Stratton,** whereas the minor road from Week St. Mary leads through Marhamchurch and eventually to Stratton. Just before Stratton to the right of the main road is the tiny rural village of *Launcells* with its lovely little parish church of St. Swithin surviving in an unrestored state.

From **Bude** the choice is either to return to **Camelford** by the coast roads as Route 3 or, if time is short, directly down the A39. In either case turn off A39 on to A395 to return via Wilsey Down and Pipers Pool to join A30 at Kennards House.

Route 5   Bodmin Moor (Route B)

From **Launceston** (by-pass) take B3254 southwards. This road will take you towards the middle of Bodmin Moor and some very fine moorland views will be seen away to the right. At Darley Ford or Upton Cross turn right towards the moors to visit the Cheesewring, the Hurlers and Caradon Hill, going on also to Siblyback and the reservoir. From Siblyback follow signs to Draynes Bridge, Redgate and beautiful Golitha Falls. Retracing route slightly, follow signs to *St. Cleer,* passing King Doniert's Stones. All southbound signposts then lead to **Liskeard.** From Liskeard follow A390 to Dobwalls and thence the Glynn Valley Road (A38) as far as Halfway House. At Halfway House turn sharply to the right towards the village of *St. Neot.* From the crossroads on Goonzion Downs one can see in the distance to the north-west remote and yet romantic Warleggan, made somewhat notorious in the 1930s by an eccentric vicar.

After visiting St. Neot, famous for its stained glass, drive northwards, taking road signposted Bolventor, over Brown Gelly Downs to visit Dozmary Pool. A good road will take you to Bolventor and Jamaica Inn to return to Launceston by A30.

Route 6   The Tamar Valley

Take the A388 to *Callington* and then follow Route 6 **(Liskeard).**

Return from Liskeard to **Launceston** on B3254.

BODMIN

The ancient county and assize town of **Bodmin** is a very proud place indeed and its development during the last decade has been most marked. It is a good centre from which to tour the whole of Cornwall, being almost in the middle of the county. Both the north and south coasts are in easy reach, eastwards is the great expanse of Bodmin Moor, and **Truro** and the gateway to West Cornwall are less than an hour's journey away.

The history of Bodmin goes back more than fifteen hundred years even before the coming of St. Petroc. Its name, Bodmin or Bod-manach, means the abode of monks. In 1295 it returned two Burgesses to Edward III's Parliament and when the Black Prince became the first Duke of Cornwall in 1337, Bodmin was the only town in the county with more than one hundred houses. It also had an important Priory Church which was one of those considered along with St. Columb and St. Mary's, Truro, for possible conversion to a cathedral for the restored Bishopric in 1877.

During the Civil War Bodmin remained loyal to the King, although at the beginning of the 17th century it was a centre of Puritanism. Since 1835 it was regarded as the county town of Cornwall when it replaced Launceston the ancient capital, and from 1838 to the comparatively recent abolition of assizes it was also the assize town.

St. Petroc's Church has many interesting features including the Norman font, and St. Petroc's casket. Bodmin Beacon, a 44 m (144 ft) high obelisk erected in 1853 in memory of a distinguished soldier, Sir Walter Raleigh Gilbert, dominates the town.

Bodmin barracks, formerly the depot of the County Regiment, the Duke of Cornwall's Light Infantry, has now been converted for industrial and trading purposes and since the absorption of the D.C.L.I. into the Light Infantry Brigade only a museum now remains. This museum can be visited and is situated in the old Keep of the Barracks. Bodmin Jail in Berrycombe Road was built during the Napoleonic Wars by prisoners and has a grim and grisly story to tell. It is now partially in ruins, and although one part has been converted into a nightclub and entertainment centre, the tall central tower still dominates that part of the town.

At the old railway station there is an interesting museum sponsored by the Great Western Society which has some rolling stock and locomotives, evocative of the halcyon days of steam and the old Great Western Railway.

Just outside Bodmin amid rolling parklands and a beautiful situation is Lanhydrock House, now the property of the National Trust. This magnificent reminder of the Victorian era must not be missed and more information will be found in the gazetteer section under the village heading of *Lanhydrock*.

Bodmin is so centrally situated that nearly all the recommended day and half-day routes radiate from the town as can be seen from the following joining instructions.

Route 1   Bodmin Moor   (Route A)
From **Bodmin** take A389 (signposted **Wadebridge**) as far as Lane End. Fork right on to B3266 through Pencarrow woods towards *St. Tudy*, and Michaelstow to join A39 for **Camelford** at Valley Truckle. Then follow Route 1 (Camelford).

Return over Bodmin Moor (A30) turning right for *Blisland* and enter Bodmin on minor roads through Helland.

Route 2   King Arthur's Country and the Camel Coast
As Route 1 **(Bodmin)** to **Camelford** then follow Route 2 (Camelford).

Return from **Wadebridge** via Egloshayle and Dunmere Valley road (A389) to Bodmin.

Route 3   Bude and The North
As Route 1 **(Bodmin)** to **Camelford,** then follow Route 3 (Camelford), returning from Camelford to Bodmin the same way.

Route 5   Bodmin Moor (Route B)
Leave **Bodmin** by A30 to **Launceston** and then follow Route 5 (Launceston). Return either from Jamaica Inn (Bolventor) over A30 or, after visiting *St. Neot,* retrace your route to Goonzion cross-roads and return to Bodmin via Warleggan, Mount and Cardinham.

Route 6   Tamar Valley
Take A38 from **Bodmin** eastward to **Liskeard** and then follow Route 6 (Liskeard), returning by the same Glynn Valley road.

Route 7   Rame Peninsula and Mount Edgecumbe Country Park
Take A38 to **Liskeard** and follow Route 7 (Liskeard).
    Return from Liskeard to **Bodmin** the same way.

Route 8   Looe, Fowey Estuary and Lanhydrock House
Take A38 from **Bodmin** through the Glynn Valley and then follow scenic route signs to **Looe.** Then follow Route 8 **(Liskeard)** returning via the Glynn Valley from Dobwalls.

Route 9   Padstow and North Coast
To join this route take the A389 to **Wadebridge,** returning from **Newquay** via A392 to Indian Queens and A30 or **St. Columb Major** then A3059 Class III road for A30 at Goss Moor.

Route 11   Truro and Roseland Peninsula
To use this route follow A30 via Fraddon, *Summercourt* and Mitchell to Carland Cross, then join A3076 for **Truro.**
    Return from **St. Austell** using A391.

Route 12   The China-Clay Countryside
Join this route at St. Blazey (B3269) and return to **Bodmin** from **St. Austell** on A391.

EAST CORNWALL

Where the River Fowey enters the sea between Polruan and the town of **Fowey** itself would seem to be a natural boundary for the East Cornwall section, but this has been extended a little farther to the west. This enables Fowey, the important town of **St. Austell,** and the entire seaboard of St. Austell Bay, which also comes within what is now the Borough of Restormel, and the attractive resorts of **Mevagissey** and Portmellon, to be included in the same section.

This eastern part of Cornwall forms the lower slopes of Bodmin Moor and then descends through very beautiful and fertile valleys to the English Channel coast. Nearer the middle of Cornwall, Bodmin Moor hardens into the granite uplands which time has decomposed to form china-clay. So, rather unexpectedly, we have a highly industralised complex with very considerable urbanisation, but nevertheless still following the same contour pattern and sloping down towards the south coast.

The holiday centres in East Cornwall, apart from the Rame peninsula and the area of Whitesand Bay, are centred around Looe, Fowey, and Mevagissey, the most attractive fishing port, west of the china-clay capital of St. Austell.

St. Austell itself and one other inland town, **Liskeard,** are suggested as touring centres. **Saltash** and Torpoint are also good centres from which to explore their rather restricted, but nonetheless interesting, localities.

Perhaps the term East Cornwall is somewhat of a misnomer. Really this is South-East Cornwall, because the very attractive stretch of coastline from Mevagissey right up to Plymouth forms almost half of Cornwall's south coast, bordering the English Channel.

The calmer waters of the English Channel provide much better facilities for boating than on the opposite coast, although of course the landlocked waters of the Camel Estuary and St. Ives Bay are two exceptions. Against this there is practically no surf on the south coast and the surf sports are non-existent, but here the small boat pursuits and water-skiing and other activities which require placid waters really come into their own.

LOOE

Looe is really two towns in one. The old boroughs of East and West Looe either side of the estuary of the River Looe are linked by an extremely fine seven-span bridge which forms a most attractive background. It is an absolute paradise for those who wish to take to the water. The reasonably long estuary gives a sense of confidence when one embarks on a fishing trip or a pleasure cruise and one is well out to sea before becoming aware of even a gentle swell.

Looe has a lot to offer the visitor. The fine sandy beaches, particularly Hannafore and Main Beaches, are safe at practically all states of the tide, and its waterfront and narrow streets possess the charm found only in communities where generations have followed the trades of the sea.

The Banjo Pier is an attractive feature of the harbour, which always presents a bustling, colourful scene full of all manner of boats from the gaily painted fishing smacks and the business-like crab and lobster boats to the sleeker lines of the yachts and speedboats.

One of the principal attractions is, of course, fishing, and shark-fishing is pre-eminent. Indeed, Looe is the headquarters of the British Shark Fishing Association and regularly massive sharks are caught and brought in to be weighed and then photographed along with the delighted angler.

The older part of the town is on the eastern bank where, among narrow winding streets, are found the old Guildhall (now a museum) and the 17th-century Jolly Sailors Inn. Principally, however, the town now consists of modern shops and cafés—always a welcome sight to the hungry visitor. Accommodation of all types abounds. The hotels of West Looe overlook the harbour with others along the edge of the cliff towards the open sea.

There is a marine aquarium on the quay in East Looe, a second 'Cornish' museum in Lower Street, East Looe, and, quite amazingly a woolly monkey colony at Murraytown on the outskirts. As one would expect Looe has a regatta, normally held on the late summer bank holiday, and a sea angling festival coinciding with the appropriate tide in mid-September. The wooded slopes and tree-covered cliffs present a quasi-continental appearance and, apart from being a good centre from which to explore its lovely river valley, Looe is a good place to spend a holiday.

The River at Looe

Banjo Pier, Looe

FOWEY

This superbly situated town, with its splendid waterfront on the west bank of the Fowey River, is probably one of the oldest ports in Great Britain. As long ago as 200 B.C. **Fowey** was on the overland pilgrim way from Ireland to the Mediterranean and during the Crusades of the 11th, 12th and 13th centuries it equipped a number of expeditions to the Holy Land. Forty-seven ships sailed from Fowey in 1346 to help besiege Calais but 32 years later, in 1378, the French revenged themselves by burning the town and slaughtering the inhabitants. During the Civil War on the Gribbin Peninsula, just outside Fowey, some 6,000 Roundheads surrendered to the Royalists.

To recapture something of the authentic atmosphere of Fowey, one should read the book *Troy Town* written by a famous son of Fowey, Sir Arthur Quiller-Couch, which depicts the genteel, or 'cumeelfo' delights of the Fowey of a generation or so ago.

Like most Cornish towns, Fowey has its seasonal traffic problems. Its narrow streets were not designed to cope with today's motorcades so it is really best to explore Fowey on foot. Visit the parish church of St. Fimbarrus, the Town Quay with the King of Prussia Hotel, named after John Carter, a notorious smuggler who haunted Prussia Cove further down the coast, Readymoney Cove, St. Catherine's Point, the Esplanade, the 17th-century almshouses, Cob's well, the 14th-century block houses at the harbour entrance and Noah's Ark in Fore Street, a most interesting and unique museum.

One of the easily accessible, simple pleasures is a trip on the ferry across to Bodinnick on the eastern bank, or slightly further away, the upper reaches of the pretty wooded river around St. Winnow, Lerryn and St. Veep are superb for exploring.

MEVAGISSEY

Mevagissey is basically a fishing port and the things that smack of the sea are readily discernible as one walks around the quays of this most fascinating place, superbly set in St. Austell Bay. A hundred years ago some ten thousand men were employed in the Cornish fishing industry but by 1967 this had declined to only five hundred. Italy provided a ready market for thousands of tons of Cornish pilchards and, indeed, this almost insatiable appetite for the principal catch gave rise to the Cornish toast:

'Here's a health to the Pope, may he live to repent,
And add six more weeks to the term of his Lent,
And teach all his vassals from Rome to the poles,
There's nothing like pilchards for saving their souls.'

The pilchard export drive over, it is perhaps fortunate that Mevagissey has the vital ingredients to make it a tourist and holiday centre.

In common with other holiday centres in Cornwall, Mevagissey's narrow streets make driving nightmarish even in broad daylight and walking, although also a hazardous business, is positively the only way to get about.

Mevagissey also is a major shark-fishing centre and there are boatmen in abundance who are prepared to give the visitor a good day's sport either way—out in the Channel angling for the big fish, or on what is sometimes rather contemptuously called the 'mackerel run', just a mile or so offshore to catch smaller fish.

A folk museum on East Quay, an aquarium and a model railway are really the only man-made attractions because the appeal of Mevagissey lies in its situation, its harbour and sheltered wooded hinterland underlining it as one of the three places on this part of the coast meriting consideration as a holiday centre.

LISKEARD

The former borough of **Liskeard** is one of the principal market towns of Cornwall and is probably about the best inland centre from which to explore the southeast corner of Cornwall. Unfortunately its hotel facilities, whilst good in themselves, are somewhat limited and this tends to deter people from using it as a touring centre.

It is, however, ideally placed. To the north and east lie some very pleasant parts of the moor where one can explore the delights of Caradon, visit interesting old villages such as *St. Cleer* or Pensilva and be in the midst of some of the finest scenery in the county. From Liskeard the

Mevagissey Harbour

valley runs through such picturesque places are *St. Keyne* towards **Looe** and the superb Glynn Valley follows the course of the River Fowey meandering through some fine scenery past Restormel and Respryn to St. Winnow and St. Veep and, ultimately, to the open sea.

It is worth mentioning that the history of Liskeard, or Liskerret which means 'court of the free cattle', goes back to the Domesday Book. Liskeard was a coinage and stannary town and during the period when the copper mines on Caradon were in production, was a very prosperous place.

It is, however, as a centre for touring South-East Cornwall that Liskeard finds its place in this list and consequently the suggested routes are confined to this part of the county.

Route 6   The Tamar Valley

From **Liskeard** travel east on the A390 through the village of *St. Ive* (where the famous Bishop Trelawney was once the vicar) to the market town of *Callington*. From Callington the road continues through interesting countryside to Gunnislake at the head of the beautiful and fertile Tamar Valley.

A good minor road can then be followed to *Calstock*, after which comes Cotehele House (q.v.) and the charming little village of *St. Dominick*. The road to Halton Quay follows a tributary of the River Tamar with Pentillie Castle to the south amid wooded parkland. A choice of roads then leads to **Saltash** from which, if desired, a visit can be made to Plymouth simply by crossing the Tamar Bridge. From Saltash the direct return route to Liskeard is via A38 (St. Germans Church and Trematon Castle can both be visited by making simple left-hand diversions off the main road).

If it is decided to visit Plymouth, the return journey to Liskeard can be made via the *Torpoint* Ferry and any selected parts of Route 10.

An alternative drive from St. Dominick is to cross the A388 and from the little village of St. Mellion proceed to *Pillaton,* where the Weary Friar Inn is noteworthy, and then to follow the wooded valley of the River Lynher to Landrake (A38).

Route 7   The Rame Peninsula and Mount Edgcumbe Country Park

Take the A38 from **Liskeard** eastwards to Trerulefoot roundabout following A38 signed Plymouth and **Saltash.** Turn right at the foot of Heskyn Hill to *St. Germans.* After looking at the church and village continue on this road to rejoin A374. Turn left and follow the main road through Sheviock and *Antony,* then take the second right-hand turning to St. John and Millbrook. The road to Cremyll skirts the Mount Edgcumbe Country Park with its superb views of Plymouth Sound and the Hamoaze. The villages of Kingsand and Cawsand overlooking Cawsand Bay can be visited on the return journey which follows the coast road overlooking Whitesand Bay to Crafthole, with its quaint Finnygook Inn, and Portwrinkle.

Return along the coast road B3247 over Battery Cliffs to *Downderry* and Seaton Bridge.

A scenically beautiful diversion can be made by following the B3247 along the valley of the River Seaton to Hessenford, turning left to join the A387. The road then crosses Bin Down (where there is an 18 hole golf course) and enters **Looe** following the valley of the East Looe River.

The return journey to Liskeard is made on B3254 via Duloe and the *St. Keyne* Valley.

Route 8   Looe, The Fowey Estuary and Lanhydrock

Follow B3254 through the *St. Keyne* Valley to **Looe.** From Looe the A387 leads directly to *Polperro* but some may prefer to use the coast road via Talland Bay. A series of well-signed minor roads leads past the wonderful Lantivet Bay towards the beautifully situated church of Lanteglos and the village of Polruan on the **Fowey** Estuary.

A leisurely drive through St. Veep, Lerryn and St. Winnow, following the river Fowey leads to *Lostwithiel* and historic Restormel Castle.

The B3268 via Sweetshouse and Trebyan will take you to Lanhydrock House and Park. After visiting this great house take the eastern drive out, turning right past the lodge to Respryn Bridge. Take the next left fork across Bofarnel Down (an extension of Braddock or Broadoak Down, a Civil War battlefield) to join the A390 and return to **Liskeard** via the villages of West, Middle and East Taphouse and Dobwalls (junction with A38).

This route can also be used as an extension of Route 7.

ST. AUSTELL

The landscape around **St. Austell** is dominated for 70 sq km (27 sq miles) by the huge pyramid-shaped tips of waste products from the lifeblood industry of this part of the county, china-clay, which presents a strange and almost science-fiction panorama to the casual visitor. Some people find these vast man-made hills offensive, but others accept them as reflecting the way of life in this area centred on the important and busy town of St. Austell.

Alas, St. Austell boasts a singularly insufficient number of hotels for its size and therefore cannot really be called a holiday centre, but with so many other amenities and facilities nearby, it has to be included as a suggested touring centre.

Originally, St. Austell consisted of a few very narrow streets around the splendid parish church of the Holy Trinity. Until mid-way through the 18th century it, too, was a tin-mining town, but then William Cookworthy, a Plymouth chemist, discovered that the decomposed granite known as kaolin, or china-clay, was to be found in the area in tremendous quantities. This led to the development of the county's third largest industry, after tourism and agriculture.

A unique tour of the china-clay areas around Bugle, Foxhole, Nanpean, St. Dennis and *St. Stephen* with the great pits, the industrial archaeology and, of course, the huge tips, is a never to be forgotten experience and from some of the high ground in the middle of this district the landscapes are quite breathtaking. It is possible from Hensbarrow Downs to see both coasts of Cornwall and between this high ridge and the sea on both sides are the older tips which kindly nature has now covered with golden gorse, tree lupins and mauve rhododendrons, to the greater beauty of inland Cornwall.

Arch of Lostwithiel Bridge

As St. Austell is a touring centre and there is really so much to see in its surrounding countryside, the other parts of the former Borough of St. Austell-with-Fowey, which now forms the industrial, southern section of Restormel District, must also be mentioned.

From the roundabout at the eastern end of the by-pass, a road leads to Charlestown, a little port with Georgian cottages and a very small dock. An esplanade runs eastward to one of Cornwall's most attractive residential estates at Carlyon Bay which overlooks Crinnis Beach. There is a golf course and the well known Carlyon Bay Hotel has a holiday and amenities complex at the eastern end of the esplanade. There are a number of interesting little harbours, coves and places of interest in this particular vicinity such as Porthpean, Ropehaven and Pentewan which is a delightful little village, now very much given over to tourism, with a large caravan site on the beach near where the White River (so called because of its high china-clay content), joins the sea.

Four tours are particularly recommended using St. Austell as a starting place.

Route 10   Lanhydrock House, Looe, The Fowey Estuary

From **St. Austell** take the A397 northwards through the eastern part of the china-clay countryside and such mining villages as Ruddlemoor, Carthew and Stenalees to Bugle. Continue on A391 over Conce Moor to Reperry Fork. Turn right on to the minor road and, crossing the high ground north of Helman Tor, arrive at the west gate of Lanhydrock House. After visiting Lanhydrock leave by the eastern drive, turn right past the lodge for Respryn Bridge. Fork left to cross Bofarnel Down (see Route 8). After joining A390, turn right on to B3359. A pleasant diversion can be made off this road to Lanreath with its ancient church and picturesque Punch Bowl Inn. From Lanreath a direct route leads to Bodinnick. From Bodinnick the car ferry will return you to **Fowey** and thence via the A3082 to Par, past the great expanse of Par Sands with its caravans and chalet parks. The A3082 and a diversion around Carlyon Bay will give superb views of St. Austell Bay as you return to base.

An alternative from Lanreath is to return to B3359 for Pelynt to join A387 at Barcelona Cross near Sclerder Abbey. Turning left will take you to **Looe** and thence back via A387 and B3254 (*St. Keyne* valley road) to **Liskeard.** Return to St. Austell via A38 to Dobwalls and A390 through *Lostwithiel* and St. Blazey. A right turn at Barcelona Cross leads to *Polperro* and thence past Lantivet Bay and Lantic Bay to Polruan on the Fowey Estuary. Return, following the river, through St. Veep, Lerryn and Lostwithiel to A390 and St. Austell.

Route 11   Truro and the Roseland Peninsula

The A390 is a direct road to **Truro** via *Probus.* From Truro there are two ways of entering the Roseland Peninsula. The first of these is via A39 (sign-posted **Falmouth**) to Playing Place, then turn left past Trelissick Gardens to the car ferry at King Harry Passage. **St. Mawes** is reached via *St. Just* and all the other places in the Roseland Peninsula (q.v.) are within easy

Lanhydrock House

reach. Return via *Veryan,* Port Holland, and the coast road, which passes Caerhayes Castle, to Gorran (Gorran Haven), Portmellon, **Mevagissey** and Pentewan Sands (B3273) to **St. Austell.**

The alternative is to return from Truro on A39 as far as Tresillian Bridge. By the church take the minor road signposted Merthyr and, driving almost parallel to the splendid wooded drive to Tregothnan Mansion, follow signs to St. Michael Penkevil and Lamorran. From Lamorran aim for Ruanlanihorne and the minor roads overlooking the Fal estuary to Philleigh, St. Just and St. Mawes.

Return to St. Austell via coast road as above.

Route 12   The China-Clay Countryside

From **St. Austell** drive east along the A390 to St. Blazey and thence up the *Luxulyan* valley past Prideaux and into the Treffry Woods. After the wooded valley the countryside changes enormously as one goes through Treverbyn to the A391. Turn right into the village of Bugle and then left following the signs to *Roche,* passing as you approach the village the unique granite mass of Roche Rock. At the top of the village by the parish church, turn left and in about 1½ km (1 mile), fork right to go over Hensbarrow Downs, 313 m (1026 ft). At the crossroads turn right over Longstone Downs (passing the area known as America on your right) towards Foxhole. At Foxhole join B3379 for High Street and thence via A3058 through Trewoon to join A390 main road into St. Austell, passing on your left the world-famous Blackpool Clay-pit and on your right the large modern clay-dries.

Route 13   Padstow and the North Coast

Follow the B3274 over Hensbarrow Downs to *Roche,* cross the Goss Moor (A30) at Roche Cross and thence through Tregonetha to Winnards Perch.

Cross A39 and follow signs to **Padstow.** The north coast bays can then be visited as in Route 9 **(Wadebridge).**

Return from either **Newquay** direct by A392 to Quintrell Downs and then A3058 via *Summercourt*, Brighton Crossroads (A39) and *St. Stephen* to A390 and **St. Austell** or from **St. Columb Major** via B3274 and A30 via Roche.

SALTASH

Saltash is included in the list of touring centres principally because it is at the Cornwall end of the all-important Tamar Bridge (A38) which links **South-East Cornwall by road to Plymouth and South Devon.** Anyone choosing Saltash as a touring centre would also have considered the fact that from the town not only the entire *Rame* peninsula and the whole of South-East Cornwall is well within excursion distance, but so is Plymouth and the south Devon countryside.

From these remarks it must not be thought, however, that Saltash is itself an unattractive place—far from it. It is unfortunate, however, that the road bridge, important as it is as a means of communication, has tended to make it a place that people go through, rather than go to. Many old houses have disappeared, particularly along the waterfront, and as a result Saltash, which had a Charter granted in 1190, has tended to lose much of its character. Nevertheless, some interesting buildings can still be seen in the steep streets which rise from the river to the 17th-century Guildhall and the ancient parish church.

The road bridge has, of course, brought many advantages—there is much new development and amenities are provided for bathing, boating and yachting in the estuary, which is also the starting place for some pleasant river excursions both up and down-stream.

SOUTH CORNWALL

The wooded estuaries of the rivers Fal, Truro and Helford which flow into **Falmouth** Bay, together with the hinterland presided over by the cathedral town of Truro form but one of the attractive areas which make up South Cornwall.

To the east of the River Fal lies the beautiful and fertile Roseland Peninsula—splendid farmland surrounded by magnificent coastline with a number of pretty villages. The northern section consists mainly of open moorland, part of the old Mining Division, and the uplands of Carnmarth with a number of small villages surrounded by the industrial remains of the once prosperous tin-mining concerns. Scattered over a wide area are the ruined mine engine-houses, count houses, shafts and chimneys, now reminders of an age that is past.

South and west of **Helston** lies the Lizard Peninsula and the Mount's Bay seaboard. The open moorland of Goonhilly Downs lies in the middle of this southerly peninsula surrounded by farming communities and the contrasting coastline bordering the English Channel.

'All roads lead to **Truro**', was a local saying during the early part of this century and so perhaps it is fitting that our tour of south Cornwall should start there.

TRURO

Truro was granted city status in 1877 as a result of the restoration of the Cornish Bishopric and the formation of the Diocese of Truro. Edward White Benson, who was its first Bishop, later became the Archbishop of Canterbury and returned in that capacity to dedicate the nave of J. L. Pearson's splendid Victorian-Gothic Cathedral whose three spires dominate the city. Although not yet 100 years old, Truro Cathedral is well worth visiting and contains much of interest.

Since the end of the last century, Truro, always an important centre of trade and commerce, has become very much the capital of Cornwall. The County Museum in River Street contains a very fine cross-section of Cornish history from the earliest times.

In 1904 Truro became the centre of administration for the county and an imposing granite-faced County Hall was built near the railway station. To house the ever-growing number of administrators, an even more imposing 'new' County Hall was built during the 1960s on a splendid site not far from its predecessor which is still in use.

Truro has its heroes, among them Richard Lander, explorer of the Niger, whose statue now loftily surveys Lemon Street with its beautiful Georgian houses. Truro's main short-coming as a tourist centre is that there are too few hotels. The Royal Hotel in Lemon Street and the Brookdale Hotel in Tregolls Road are supplemented by a number of smaller hotels and guest houses, but if Truro is really to succeed as a touring centre, and perhaps it does not either need or want to, there is scope for two more first-class hotels. Truro is nevertheless a good centre from which to explore this part of Cornwall. **Falmouth** and West Cornwall are within easy reach and the delightful Roseland Peninsula is not very far away, as will be found in the first of the recommended routes.

Route 15   The Roseland Peninsula
From Truro drive eastward along A39 and then A390 via *Probus* to **St. Austell** then follow Route 15 **(St. Columb)** to Mevagissey for your sight-seeing journey through the Roseland.

An alternative return route is via Ruanlanihorne, Lamorran Woods and Merthyr rejoining A39 at Tresillian.

Route 16   Perranporth, the North Cliffs and the Mining Division
Leave **Truro** on the B3284 crossing the A30 at Chybucca Cross to join the A3075. Follow left-fork signs for **Perranporth.** Leave Perranporth on B3284 over Trevellas Downs, the headquarters of the Cornish Gliding and Flying Club, to *St. Agnes,* from there the coast road can be followed (except near Nancekuke) to the B3300 for Portreath. Continue by following

the B3301 over Reskageage Downs (the North Cliffs) past Hell's Mouth.

In a mile the road crosses the Red River and a diversion to the right to Godrevy Towans (National Trust) with a fine view of the lighthouse and of **St. Ives** Bay is well worth taking.

Near Gwithian Church fork left to join the A30 east of Connor Downs. The direct return route follows A30 through **Camborne** (by-pass opening sometime in 1975) and the industrial areas of Tuckingmill, Pool and Illogan Highway to **Redruth** by-pass to join A390 at Scorrier for Truro via Chacewater.

The 'mining division' route crosses A30 and passes through Carnhell Green to join B3280. Turn left and after crossing B3303 at Praze-an-Beeble, the road leads to the B3280 on the high ground, over 215 m (700–800 ft) above sea level, around Four Lanes. Descending through Carnmenellis the *Stithians* Reservoir comes into view and the A394 Helston–Penryn road can be seen. At the crossroads before the main road, however, fork left for Stithians and the A393. Turn left and then right for Gwennap Pit and Gwennap. The district of the old United Mines can then be seen as one goes along B3298 to Carharrack and *St. Day*. A series of minor roads lead through Crofthandy to Baldhu (Black Mine) where the comparatively new Wheal Jane enterprise is leading a resurgence of the mining industry.

From Baldhu return to Truro by well signposted roads.

Route 17   Falmouth and the Helford River
From **Truro** follow the A39 south-westwards through Carnon Downs and *Perranarworthal*. Turn left through Carclew Woods to Restonguet Creek, *Mylor* Bridge and Mylor Creek with its Pandora Inn. The road then leads to picturesque *Flushing* and past St. Gluvias church, into *Penryn* and **Falmouth**.

After visiting Falmouth, leave by the coast road (Swanpool beach and Maenporth) to Rosemullion Head (National Trust), Mawnan Smith and the Helford River (Helford Passage and the well-known Ferryboat Inn). The road then leads through some delightful scenery around Calamansac and Polwheveral Creek past Constantine to Gweek.

From Gweek this route returns the visitor to the A394 Helston–Penryn road to return directly to Truro via Treluswell cross and the A39.

If you wish to continue around the southern bank of the Helford River follow the directions given for Route 18 **(Helston)**.

ST. MAWES
St. Mawes is really little more than a village with a population of just under a thousand, yet it is the centre of activity in the delightful part of Cornwall known as the Roseland peninsula.

Blessed with a mild all-the-year-round climate (the proprietors of two hotels in St. Mawes have offered free accommodation to those staying there on any days during which the hotels are enveloped in fog or when snow falls), St. Mawes has many advantages and the landlocked areas of St.

Mawes harbour and the Percuil creek offer some of the safest boating anywhere in Britain.

There is not much beach, rather it is a stony foreshore. It is possible, however, to find some stretches of sand and shingle along the south-facing water-front on which to relax.

The harbour itself, guarded by **Henry VII's** castle—it has its twin across the estuary on Pendennis Point at **Falmouth**—provides all the facilities needed for boating and yachting. Such hotels as exist are good, and plenty of other types of holiday accommodation can be obtained in St. Mawes itself and all over the Roseland.

A word of warning, however—buses are not entirely absent, but the Roseland is basically for the motorist, the walker and of course the boat owner. August is the scheduled month of the Regatta and Carnival, but a real holiday atmosphere seems to last throughout the year.

FALMOUTH

The old part of **Falmouth** has an attraction which almost defies description. Packet ships used to put into 'Falmouth for Orders': the streets and the attractive water-front are full of the relics of the town's seafaring past and the visible signs of its seafaring present. One such relic is the rather fearsome original figurehead of H.M.S. Amazon on Upton Slip off Church Street.

Nowadays Falmouth is also an important tourist resort with a splendid sea-front, bathing beaches, a wide variety of hotels and all the usual re-creational facilities and amenities. It is, however, the atmosphere of the water-front and the harbour that pervades the whole town. Falmouth Docks play an important part in the economic life of the town and the surrounding area, and the large ships in the docks usually dominate the seascape.

Small boats proliferate and the calm waters and numerous creeks and inlets which provide safe anchorages make the world's third largest natural harbour a yachtsman's and small boat owner's paradise. The Penryn and Truro Rivers provide ample opportunities for sailing and boating, whilst the more adventurous and more experienced sailors can venture out past the St. Mawes and Pendennis Castles to the open waters of Falmouth Bay and the charms of the Helford River and beyond.

In Falmouth's long history as a port, clashes between the Revenue or Preventive men (the Customs Officers) and smugglers were a frequent occurrence, and the presence of the King's Pipe, the chimney where confiscated contraband tobacco was burned, on Custom House Quay is a reminder of those colourful days.

The important family of Killigrew lived here and Falmouth has particularly interesting Royalist associations. The 17th-century parish church in the centre of the town is one of the few dedicated in the name of Charles I, King and Martyr.

The Castle Drive is a coastal road around Pendennis Castle, from which there are splendid views of the harbour and Falmouth Bay as far southwest as the dreaded Manacle Rocks. Below is Castle Beach with numerous rock pools offering children exciting exploration at low tide. Gyllyngvase Beach, near Gyllyngdune Gardens and the Princess Pavilion (where summer shows are held) is the largest of Falmouth's four beaches, the others are at Swanpool and Maenporth.

Falmouth's Gardens are nationally famous, having won for the town the 'Britain in Bloom' title two or three times in the last five years. The Fox Rosehill Gardens (entered from Melville Road) contain over 200 species of foreign plants, and sub-tropical flowers and shrubs grow in luxuriant beauty. Kimberley Park also has many exotic trees and shrubs including the dracaena palms which give Falmouth its Mediterranean atmosphere and lend their name to the main avenue into the town.

From Prince of Wales Pier boat trips and cruises can be enjoyed upriver to **Truro,** across the harbour to **St. Mawes,** *St. Anthony-in-Roseland* and Percuil, or across the bay to the Helford River and romantic Frenchman's Creek.

Falmouth is physically joined to the ancient former borough of *Penryn* which is described in the gazetteer section.

HELSTON

The ancient Borough of **Helston** is known far and wide as 'the quaint old Cornish town' where, every year on 8th May, the 'band with the curious tone' leads the dancers as they join in the splendidly maintained tradition of celebrating the coming of summer with the Furry Dance. The delightful spectacle of the Children's Dance, followed at noon by the elegant Midday Dance attracts thousands of sightseers to Helston's narrow streets.

The Furry Dance apart, Helston is an attractive town ideally situated at the centre of the Lizard peninsula holiday area. Hotel accommodation in the town itself is rather less than adequate but there are plenty of guest houses and good bed and breakfast facilities in the area. Farmhouse accommodation, camping and caravanning are also popular in this district.

Helston owes much of its present prosperity to the close proximity of H.M.S. Seahawk—the Royal Naval Air Station at Culdrose a mile or so from the town.

The Angel Hotel in Coinagehall Street was formerly the town house of the Godolphin family and dates in part from the 16th century with an assembly room and minstrel's gallery.

A museum in the Old Butter Market building contains a variety of fascinating exhibits. It is open on weekdays from 10.30 a.m. to 12.30 p.m. and 2.00 p.m. to 4.30 p.m. (except Wednesday afternoons).

Formerly a stannary town, Helston was named in the Domesday Book as Henliston. There was also a castle which was at one period the residence of Edmund, Earl of Cornwall.

On the road from Helston to the Lizard the tourist passes the important radio and earth satellite communication station of Goonhilly with its three impressive 'dishes' maintaining a constant link with all parts of the world as well as with outer space.

Route 18   Helford, Meneage and the Lizard Peninsula

From **Helston** take the A3083 south past HMS Seahawk, RNAS Culdrose. Turn left on to B3291 (possibly using the Air Station viewing bay) to Gweek where a right turn on to B3293 will lead to the southern banks of the Helford River and in particular through St. Martin to *Manaccan* and *St. Anthony*.

From *Manaccan* a road leads south to *St. Keverne* and the B3293 (the notorious Manacles rocks are just to the seaward) for Coverack.

The B3294 and B3293 will then lead back towards Goonhilly Downs and the earth satellite station, whilst the only other road of any size leads southwest from Traboe Cross to Cadgwith, *Landewednack*, Lizard Town and the Lizard Point (the most southerly point in Great Britain).

Return either direct on the main road A3083 or via beautiful Kynance Cove, *Mullion* Village and Cove, Gunwalloe and Loe Pool.

Route 19   The West Coast

From **Helston** take the B3304 past Penrose and Loe Pool to *Porthleven* and then out to join A394 at Ashton, after visiting Rinsey (National Trust). Diversions to Prah Sands and Prussia Cove make the drive along the A394 increasingly interesting until at last St. Michael's Mount comes into breathtaking view as one enters *Marazion*.

This suggested route leads back to **Helston** via St. Hilary, with its Street-restored church, and Godolphin to *Breage*. To extend this tour to include the Lands End Peninsula follow Route 20 **(Penzance)**.

WEST CORNWALL

West of the estuary of the River Gannel lies the charming little village of Crantock, which is really part of **Newquay**, and the vast expanse of sand dunes forming the background to Holywell Bay. The north coast then continues down to the popular holiday area centred on **Perranporth** and *St. Agnes*.

The Mining Division

The old Mining Division of the county, centred on the twin towns of **Camborne** and **Redruth,** with spurs running northwards to St. Agnes and *Gwithian* and south to the Carnon Valley, forms the greater inland part of this area. In sunshine the ruined minestacks and old workings and the vast tracts of bare open countryside have a grandeur all their own. When the penetrating, but life-giving Cornish rain is driven almost horizontally across the countryside which is exposed to the full fury of the Atlantic winds, this is a bleak and forbidding land indeed.

Hayle is situated at the western edge of the mining area, after which comes the wide sweep of St. Ives Bay to the seaward and the contrasting

Penwith peninsula with its granite uplands and spectacular rocky coastline, from Navax Point right around Cape Cornwall and Lands End to Mounts Bay.

In this part of Cornwall Perranporth, Hayle and **St. Ives** are three of the recognised holiday centres, whilst Camborne and Redruth, either taken as one or as two separate towns, form a good inland touring centre. **Penzance** is indisputably both a holiday resort in its own right and the obvious choice as a centre from which to tour the Lands End, or Penwith Peninsula.

The Lands End Peninsula

Penwith is really an 'extremity' and therefore West Penwith is the western extremity of Cornwall. This area is chiefly remembered for its splendid natural scenery and its wealth of antiquities. The Penwith uplands, a line of granite hills, are a wonderful vantage point from which to appreciate the sharp contrasts provided by the stark 'carns' or granite outcrops, the fertile strip of arable fields and pasturelands, the sheer headlands and cliffs, and finally, the mighty Atlantic ocean, innocuous enough on a calm day but spectacularly awesome when stirred up by gale-force winds.

Penwith has a wide variety of prehistoric remains, some going back to the Neolithic and Bronze Ages. The great quoits or cromlechs are all remains of the tombs of chieftains, whereas the stone circles mark the places of religious or ceremonial observance. Of a later date (some 2,000 years old) are the Iron Age hill-top forts and the villages of Chysauster and Carn Euny. The Celtic influence is very marked in the pattern of scattered hamlets. Penwith's industrial past is also evident by the number of ruined mine-engine houses scattered all over the area.

PERRANPORTH

Perranporth is largely a modern town which has grown up as a result of the 'discovery' of the superb sun-bathing and surfing on the great expanse of sand which is Perranporth Beach.

The amenities of this popular resort are increasing; small guest house and bed and breakfast type accommodation abounds and there are some good hotels. Although the principal attractions are the wide open spaces of the beach, dunes and Atlantic breakers, the old parish church of Perranzabuloe, from which Perranporth originates is not without its historical interest.

It was here in A.D. 550 that St. Piran, one of the foremost preachers of the Gospel, built his Oratory. Unfortunately he built on the shifting sands and for many centuries what is believed to be the earliest known Christian church in the United Kingdom lay buried. Earlier this century it was rediscovered and a concrete shell built over the top to preserve it. At the present time further consideration is being given to the problem of safe-guarding the Oratory.

Lands End

HAYLE

Hayle is a busy town of over 6,000 population through which the A30 trunk road passes. At first sight it may seem rather a drab place but the industrial atmosphere created by the harbour and a power station is more than compensated for by the magnificent stretch of golden sand, some 5 km (3 miles) of it, forming a section of the beautiful St. Ives Bay, known as Hayle Towans. Here there are facilities for camping and caravanning and there are some good chalet parks. An attractive natural feature is the Carnsew Estuary Wildfowl and Wader Reserve. In a Plantation on the Carnsew Estate there is a Roman tombstone.

CAMBORNE-REDRUTH

Some forty years ago the twin mining towns of **Camborne** and **Redruth** were merged for local government administrative convenience in spite of fierce opposition from the residents of both towns who wished to keep their identity and independence. Since that day the towns have grown physically closer until they are to all intents and purposes a single conurbation—if that is not too grandiose a word for an urban settlement of 40,000 people. Whether the towns have grown closer together in any other way is a matter of conjecture.

Camborne-Redruth (and for purposes of this book one must consider them as one town), is a sprawling, industrialised area which formed the centre of the old West Cornwall Mining Division and nowadays plays a vitally important part in the industrial and economic life of West Cornwall.

The area abounds with relics of the past, the age of invention and the zenith of the Cornish Mining Industry. Camborne was the birthplace of Richard Trevithick who was born in 1771 and devoted his whole life to his inventions, mainly steam engines. In 1801 he drove a steam vehicle in Oxford Street, London, and his statue in Camborne shows him holding a steam engine. The inventor of the safety fuse, William Bickford, was also born in Camborne, at Trucken Mill. In a house in Redruth William Murdoch discovered coal-gas, and an air of purposeful bustle still hangs over the busy streets, factories and works yards.

Dominating the landscape of rocky Carn Brea is the obelisk memorial to Lord de Dunstanville & Basset of Tehidy, owner of many mines and generous benefactor of the miners and their families, whilst all around can be seen the ruins of the mine-engine houses (jinjies) with their crumbling chimneys evocative of the early 19th-century era of Victorian industrialism and energy. One of these old mine count houses, the Basset Count House near Carnkie just off the Redruth–Helston road, has been turned into a first-class restaurant where one can eat good food served in unique surroundings.

For those interested in mining and metallurgy the Camborne School of Mines, known throughout the world as a training centre for mining engineers, has an excellent museum; there is also the Camborne Museum and for the engineering enthusiasts the museum at the Holmans Engineering Works is full of interest.

Mention has already been made of the National Trust's exhibition of Cornish Engines at Pool, 3 km (2 miles) east of Camborne. The engines may be seen Mondays to Fridays from April to mid-October. Times of openings are usually 11 a.m.–1 p.m. and 2 p.m.–6 p.m.; any variations are displayed on notice boards.

The Royal Cauldon Potteries at Wilson Way, Camborne, are also open to the public, as is Fosters Pottery at Tolgus Hill on the outskirts of Redruth.

Hotels are few and far between—possibly Penventon at Redruth and Tyacks at Camborne are among the best—but, as in most areas of Cornwall, there is plenty of other holiday accommodation. A municipal leisure centre at Carn Brea opened last year with many recreational facilities including swimming pools, and squash courts. The Tehidy Golf Course, the vast open spaces of the North Cliffs (on the Atlantic coast) with the awesome Hell's Mouth are amenity areas to the north of the towns.

Route 16   Perranporth, the North Cliffs and the Mining Division
From **Redruth** take the A30 north-eastwards to Chybucca Cross and then follow Route 16 **(Truro).**
Return from *St. Day* to Redruth by signposted road.

Route 17   Falmouth and the Helford River
From **Redruth** take the A393 south through Lanner to Ponsanooth. Turn left in Ponsanooth (signposted **Truro**) and then join and follow A39 as far as *Perranarworthal.* Follow Route 17 (Truro) returning from Gweek over Boskenwyn Downs to cross A394 and take B3267 for Wendron and Redruth.

Route 18   Helford and the Lizard Peninsula
Route 19   The West Coast
For either route from **Redruth** or **Camborne** take nearest signposted road to **Helston,** then follow Route 18 (Helston).
Return the same way Route 19 (Helston) and from *Marazion* or **Penzance** via A30 through **Hayle** and Connor Downs.

Route 20   Lands End Peninsula
Join this route at **Penzance** from A30 via Connor Downs and **Hayle.**
Return the same way, joining A30 after leaving Lelant.

ST. IVES

St. Ives is probably one of the best known of all the Cornish resorts. Tourists have been flocking to this charming old fishing port for generations to walk through the Digey, Virgin Street, Salubrious Place or other quaintly named narrow streets and to sit on the golden sands of Porthminster, Porthmeor and Porthgwidden beaches.

The fishing industry on which the town once relied has diminished in importance, but a number of fishing boats still put out from St. Ives and it is now possible for visitors to join in some specially selected fishing trips.

Atmosphere and natural attractions apart, St. Ives has much to offer. The unique Barnes Museum of Cinematography, the St. Ives Museum at Wheal Dream and the interesting parish church of St. Ia are worth visiting, whilst the Leach Pottery (Bernard Leach the founder is a potter of international repute); Dame Barbara Hepworth's garden of sculpture, and the interesting Sloop Craft Market near the Sloop Inn which has been in existence since 1392, provide other diversions.

St. Ives is one of the two places left in Cornwall where the ancient game of hurling with the silver ball takes place annually. On Feast Monday—the Monday after 2nd February—the Mayor throws up the ball from the church yard wall and the 'uppies' and the 'downies' or those who live 'upalong' versus those who live 'downalong' scramble for possession on the sands.

Every five years on St. James Day, 26th July, a curious custom immortalising James Knill, a former Collector of Customs who died in 1872, takes place around Knill's Steeple on Worvas Hill. It involves the Mayor, the Town Clerk, the Town Fiddler, two widows and ten little girls dressed in white. This ceremony will next take place in 1976.

PENZANCE

When voyaging by land, sea or air, to or from the south-west, **Penzance** is the first and last town of any size or importance in England. West of Penzance there are about 16 km (10 miles) of the A30 left before the Lands End and some 4,000 miles of Atlantic Ocean between the Old and the New World.

Penzance is a holiday centre in its own right and an ideal touring centre from which to explore the Lands End peninsula. It boasts many amenities: it is a good centre for boating, sailing and fishing including deep-sea and shark fishing. The long stretch of beach at *Marazion* and the delights of *Mousehole* and *Newlyn* combine to make this a good place in which to spend a holiday.

The fairytale castle of St. Michael's Mount, once a Benedictine Monastery, now the property of the National Trust, rises on its rocky crag out of the waters of Mount's Bay. The Mount is open to the public every Wednesday and Friday to show the Church and Blue Drawing-Rooms (additionally on Mondays, June to September when further rooms are shown), October to May. At high tide the Mount is an island but at low tide the village and castle can be reached along the $\frac{3}{4}$ km ($\frac{1}{2}$ mile) causeway from Marazion beach.

The Nautical and Man o' War Exhibitions in Chapel Street have already been mentioned and the Royal Geological Society of Cornwall has its museum in the Guildhall in Alverton Street.

The Market House and Old Town Hall in Market Jew Street, which is noteworthy for its raised pavement, has a central dome from which fine views of the town and surrounding countryside may be obtained. Outside the building is an imposing statue of Humphry Davy, one of Penzance's famous sons, who invented the miners' safety lamp.

The Harbour, quays, quaint slips and alleyways are fun to explore and there is a very fine promenade and sea wall. The Morrab Gardens are a delight to the eye and 3 km (2 miles) north west of the town are Trengwainton Gardens. This National Trust property comprises a shrub garden and a series of walled gardens containing a superb collection of tender plants and shrubs, particularly rhododendrons. There are also fine views over Mount's Bay. The gardens are open from March to September on Wednesdays, Thursdays and Fridays and Saturdays and Bank Holiday Mondays from 11 a.m.–6 p.m.

Numbers 510 and 512 buses run from Penzance and alight at Boswednan Turn or Madron, just over 1 km ($\frac{3}{4}$ mile).

Penzance offers plenty of recreational facilities with ballrooms at St. Johns Hall, the Garden on the promenade, the Ritz Mecca in Queen Street and the Grand Casino on the promenade (seasonal). Speed Hill Climbs are held regularly at Trengwainton and the annual regatta, carnival and Corpus Christi Fair, angling festival, bowls tournament and Vintage Vehicle Rally (in July) are major events in the local calendar.

The old fishing villages of Mousehole and more particularly Newlyn have of course long been known to artists, and the picturesque views of harbour, fishquays, jetties and quaint streets and cottages have been reproduced many times with many interpretations.

Penzance is an important centre of communications as far as the Isles of Scilly are concerned. It is from Penzance that the B.A. helicopter service takes off from Eastern Green Heliport and the R.M.S. *Scillonian* maintains a weekday ferry service to St. Mary's, Isles of Scilly. The main railway line from Paddington has its Western Region terminus here and a network of country bus services serve the rural areas of Penwith. Penzance has some good hotels on the seafront, and guest houses and bed and breakfast establishments are plentiful.

Camping and caravanning facilities exist at Eastern Green and throughout the area, which inevitably gets saturated during the peak weeks. Early reservation of pitches and sites is not only desirable, but a necessity.

Route 20   Lands End Peninsula

This is probably one of the best known scenic routes in the British Isles and therefore only the brief details are given. Variations can be indulged in at will, merely by following any turning signed **Penzance.** Two of the more interesting variations are given as examples.

Leave Penzance on B3315 via *Newlyn* and, with diversions to *Paul, Mousehole* and Lamorna Cove arrive at Porthcurno. A diversion around St. Levan is interesting and the main road continues along B3315 to *Sennen* and the Lands End. A variation is to leave by A30 turning left at Catchall on to A3283 for *St. Buryan,* Porthcurno and Lands End.

From Lands End the coast road follows B3306, (leave A30 at Escalls)

St. Michael's Mount

after having first visited Sennen Cove. From *St. Just* the road leads through *Morvah* (B3300) and *Zennor* to **St. Ives** with wonderful sea views the whole way. Return to Penzance via A3074 (Carbis Bay and Lelant) and A30 (Whitecross and Crowlas).

An interesting alternative is to' turn right at Morvah and follow the minor road over the high ground past Lanyon Quoit and many other relics to Madron, Hea Moor and Penzance.

The B3311 from *Gulval* past Castle-an-Dinas, and the ancient settlement of Chysauster, through Amalbrea, Amalwhidden and Towednack provides an interesting journey between Penzance and the coast road B3300 in either direction.

THE ISLES OF SCILLY

Although nearly always linked with Cornwall in the eyes of the holiday-maker, the Isles of Scilly are in fact a completely separate entity. Some 58 km (36 miles) of one of the most turbulent areas of the Atlantic Ocean separate the islands from the Cornish coast. Legend has it, however, that this was not always so, and that at one time the Isles were linked to the mainland before a great storm engulfed the land of Lyonesse. The story goes that on stormy nights one can still hear the bells of the one hundred and forty drowned churches ringing a watery knell.

The climate of the Isles is superb and, because of the influence of the Gulf Stream, sub-tropical plants and shrubs flourish in riotous profusion. The Atlantic breezes, or, of course, in winter, the gales, tend to make the atmosphere very bracing, but the mean temperature is well above that of any part of the mainland and although frost is not entirely unknown it very rarely occurs, and appreciable snowfalls are very rare indeed.

One of the most splendid views of the 145 islands is from the air. As the British Airways helicopter approaches St. Mary's, the largest island, after only a 17 minute trip from Penzance, passengers can see the entire archipelago set out as it were in relief below them, providing an unforgettable spectacle, and leaving a lasting impression. At high water all the islands are separated but at low tide there are vast expanses of sand, and some islands appear to be joined.

Apart from St. Mary's only four other islands are now inhabited. Tresco is the next largest, with sand-surrounded St. Martin's, St. Agnes and Bryher in descending order of size. Samson, the sixth largest island is no longer inhabited and all the others are very tiny indeed.

Centuries of insular existence have bred a hardy race of independent Scillonians. Intermarriage with early settlers, raiders and, of course, the neighbouring Cornish, has not been without its influence and the visitor to the Isles will find the Islanders friendly, warm-hearted and welcoming.

St. Agnes Lighthouse

ST. MARY'S

St. Mary's, the largest of the Isles, is some 4 km (2½ miles) long and 2 km (1½ miles) wide. Hugh Town, the 'capital', stands astride a sandy isthmus between the two main hills. To the north is St. Mary's Pool, the harbour, and on the other side the delightful bathing beach known as Porth Cressa.

Approaching St. Mary's from the seaward, the visitor's eye is immediately drawn to Star Castle on the top of Garrison Hill above the Quay. An Elizabethan garrison, built in 1593 for Sir Francis Godolphin, its name derives from its star-shape. The castle has been used as a prison —Prince Charles took refuge there during the Civil War—and the dwelling-house, which is also star-shaped, is now a hotel.

Not far away from Hugh Town is Old Town, originally the Town of St. Mary's. Only a few stones remain of the ancient church but the beautiful churchyard is the last resting place of many sailors and their wives.

In 1707 H.M.S. *Association,* carrying Admiral of the Fleet Sir Cloudesley Shovel, was wrecked off the Isles while on its way home from taking part in the capture of Gibraltar. The Admiral was drowned and his body was washed ashore and buried at Porth Hellick, where there is still a rough monument in his memory. Later on, his remains were disinterred and he now lies among the nation's heroes in Westminster Abbey.

There are a number of ancient burial places and granite tombs on the island, many dating from the Bronze Age, and some which still await excavation. There are historical burial chambers at Bant's Cave and Innisidgen.

Antiquities apart, it is mainly the quality of life and the atmosphere of peace and tranquillity that attracts visitors to the Isles of Scilly. There is some excellent holiday accommodation on St. Mary's, but, of course, the very size of the island indicates that it is limited and in great demand, especially in the peak period. Hugh Town has a cinema, a club, tennis courts, shops, a 9 hole golf course and other amenities.

The outstanding attraction of a holiday here, as other islands is, of course, the lure of the sea. Boat trips to the off islands can easily be arranged, as can fishing expeditions. Fresh lobsters, crayfish and other delicacies are well worth sampling and can usually be obtained at all the restaurants and hotels.

TRESCO

Tresco is almost world-famous for its superb gardens. As has been said before, the climate permits luxuriant sub-tropical shrubs and plants to blossom freely and these, together with masses of blooms of the indigenous rhododendrons and azaleas, or in spring, the daffodils, narcissi and other bulbs, provide a botanical spectacle of such riotous colour that it is not easily forgotten.

Having regard to the splendid natural beauty of the island, it is hardly surprising that ever since Augustus Smith, the great benefactor and organiser of the Islands, built the comparatively modern Abbey House, Tresco has been the home of the Lord Proprietor.

A wall and cloister arches still remain of the 12th-century St. Nicholas Abbey built here by the monks of Tavistock. The cresset from the St. Agnes Light is preserved in the garden. One of the features of the island is Valhalla, where there are a great number of intriguing figure-heads from ships wrecked off the island's sometimes inhospitable shores. Cromwell's Castle guarding the north of the island and overlooking the sea passage between Tresco and Bryher was built in the 17th century.

ST. MARTIN'S

This is an island of contradictions. Some 3 km (2 miles) in length, the sunny south-facing slopes are highly cultivated and the early flowers are a remarkable contrast to the starker eastern and northern fringes exposed to the full force of the Atlantic gales.

On St. Martin's stands Daymark Tower, nearly 12 m (40 ft) high. This was built in 1637 to guide seafarers and, standing nearly 49 m (160 ft) above sea level, it is visible for many miles. 16 km (10 miles) to the north-east are the Seven Stones, seven jagged rocks only visible at the lower states of the tide which are a menace to shipping. The ill-fated oil tanker Torrey Canyon ran aground on this reef in 1967 in spite of the Seven Stones Lightship, which has been warning sailors of the reef's hazards since 1851.

BRYHER

Lying 5 km (3 miles) from St. Mary's and to the west of Tresco, Bryher possesses some of the finest scenery to be found in the islands. Bulb fields proliferate on the south-facing slopes, and as on St. Martin's, the north of the island is wilder and barren. Shipman Head, a rocky outcrop some

Valhalla, Tresco Gardens

30 m (100 ft) high, is separated from the main island by a cleft through which the Atlantic forces its way in a spectacular manner. Bryher has many rocky clefts which provide nesting places for a number of species of sea birds.

The aptly named Hell Bay has seen the wreck of many fine ships in its troubled waters. 1½ km (1 mile) out in the open sea lies the diminutive Scilly Rock which gives its name to the entire group.

ST. AGNES

St. Agnes is about 1½ km (1 mile) south-west of St. Mary's and is reached by crossing what is known as the Sound. The island's quay is at Porth Conger near the old Coastguard Watch. Of much interest to visitors is The Gugh, a separate island at high tide but joined to St. Agnes at low water. There are some megalithic remains on The Gugh, a 3 m (9 ft) high stone monolith known as the Old Man of Gugh, and a farm house. The uninhabited island of Annet to the west of St. Agnes, is a sandy area noted as the breeding ground of puffins. There are many dangerous reefs and rocks to the west, the lonely nesting grounds of multitudes of sea birds. St. Agnes also has a Bird Observatory, from which many interesting discoveries have been made about bird migration.

The well known Bishop Rock Lighthouse guards the exposed Western Isles and sends its warning light to sailors using the western approaches.

SAMSON

This island is no longer inhabited although it was lived on from prehistoric times until the mid-19th century, as evidenced by the number of barrows. In 1836 explorations and excavations revealed a good example of a kistvaen.

Puffins and sea birds

GAZETTEER

ALTARNUN (pop. 650) is an attractive little moorland village lying just off the A30. The fine church of St. Nonna stands in the centre of the village overlooking Penpont Water. At nearby Trewint is a cottage formerly the home of Digory Isbell and his wife, where John Wesley used to stay regularly. Over the entrance of the Methodist Chapel is a statue of Wesley carved by Neville Northey Burnard the Launceston sculptor. On the A30 at Bolventor is the famous Jamaica Inn, reputed haunt of smugglers, and made famous by Daphne du Maurier's novel. *The nearest market town and bus depot is Launceston.*

ANTONY is a small village near Torpoint on the A374. The parish church of St. James contains an interesting canopied brass memorial to Margery Arundell as well as a monument to Richard Carew (died 1620) author of *A Survey of Cornwall.* The church of Maryfield stands in the grounds of Antony House (see page 91). *Nearest town and bus depot—Torpoint; Nearest station—Plymouth (North Road).*

BLISLAND which lies just off the A30 is one of the few Cornish villages having a village green surrounded by tall elms and granite cottages with slate roofs. The church of St. Proetus (or Pratt) and St. Hyacinth contains a painted screen and many other interesting features. St. Pratt's Fair is held annually on the Monday following the nearest Sunday to 25th September. *The nearest town and bus depot is Bodmin; Nearest station—Bodmin Road.*

BODMIN (pop. 9260) a former borough and County Assize town is a touring centre ideally situated at the junction of the A30 and the A38, in the middle of the county (see page 43) and is on bus routes. The parish church, the Regimental Museum of the former D.C.L.I., and Lanhydrock House and Park are of special interest. *Information Office—Priory House; Early closing day—Wednesday; Market day—Saturday; Nearest station—Bodmin Road.*

BOSCASTLE (pop. 583) is a delightful fishing village attractively situated on the B3263 where the Valency river meets the Atlantic Ocean. The Harbour and much of the magnificent coastline belongs to the National Trust, which has an Information Centre here. The two churches, Forrabury and Minster, are interesting; and of the principal hotels, the Napoleon and the Wellington are reminders of the Napoleonic Wars. The Boscastle coach used to leave the Wellington Hotel for Newquay. There is a Museum of Witchcraft. The village has many cottage industries including the making of sweets, jams and other preserves as well as a pottery and a candlemakers. *Nearest town and bus depot—Camelford; Nearest station—Bodmin Road.*

BREAGE is a not unattractive village on the A394 and bus route between Falmouth and Helston. Godolphin House, part of which dates from the 16th century, was the home of one of Cornwall's most influential families. Around the sea-girt Rinsey Mine (NT property) the cliff and coastal scenery is very beautiful. The nearest beaches are Prah Sands, Rinsey and Keneggy.

BUDE (pop. 4000) is an Atlantic Coast resort town and holiday centre on the A39 (see page 26) and bus routes. The principal beaches are Summerleaze, Crooklets, Northcott Mouth and Widemouth Bay. *Early closing day—Thursday; Information Office—The Castle; Nearest station—St. Davids' Exeter (Devon) (thence by coach).*

CALLINGTON (pop. 2647) is an inland town at the junction of the A388 and A390 almost equidistant from Launceston, Tavistock, Liskeard and Saltash. Dupath Well is regarded as being the best preserved of all the Cornish Holy Wells. From the summit of Kit Hill 325 m (1067 ft), fine views of the surrounding countryside can be obtained. *Market day—Wednesday; Early closing day—Thursday; Nearest main line station—Liskeard.*

CALSTOCK is the village centre of a large and scattered parish (pop. 4000), comprising a number of villages including Gunnislake on the A390 into Cornwall from Devon, St. Ann's Chapel, Chilsworthy, Albaston and Harrowbarrow. The 15th century Cotehele House, 3 km (2 miles) away, is open daily mornings and afternoons, April to mid-October. The house has some fine furniture, tapestries and armour of the Earls of Mount Edgcumbe. Calstock is the centre of the wonderfully fertile Tamar Valley famous for early fruit, especially strawberries, flowers and vegetables. The Tamar Valley museum contains relics of past industries, shipbuilding and mining. A Shell/National Trust Nature Trail starts at Cotehele Quay.

Across the river in Devon is Morwellham Quay a centre for recreation and education. *Nearest town and bus depot Callington; Nearest station—Plymouth (North Road).*

CAMBORNE (pop. 14,952) on the A30, is the westernmost partner in the urbanised area of Camborne-Redruth (see page 63). There are museums and much industrial archaeology. The nearest beaches are Portreath, Godrevy and Hayle Towans. *Early closing day—Thursday; Market day—Friday; Information Office—Municipal Office, Camborne; Bus and train services are frequent from Camborne.*

CAMELFORD (pop. 1220) is a small town and touring centre on the A39 (see page 32) and is on the bus route. Its proximity to the coast and moors are the chief attraction. *Early closing day—Wednesday; Information Office—Council Office, College Road; Nearest station—Bodmin Road.*

CUBERT (pop. 500) is a small village just off the A3075 on the periphery of the Newquay holiday area. It is on a bus route and there is a magnificent stretch of sandy beach with good surfing conditions at Holywell Bay (National Trust). Among the interesting old houses in the area are Ellenglaze Manor, Chynoweth Farm and Carines Farm which had a bedroom and a sitting-room built especially for John Wesley's private use. *Nearest town, bus depot, station and airport—Newquay.*

DELABOLE (pop. 1200) is a rather bleak and forbidding village on the high ground B3314 between the moors and the sea. The Old Delabole Slate Quarries are interesting and can be visited. *Nearest* *station—Bodmin Road; Nearest towns and bus depots—Wadebridge and Camelford.*

DOWNDERRY is a small seaside village on the B3247 forming a community with Hessenford and Seaton. Situated in a delightful valley this area is very popular with holidaymakers especially caravanners and campers. The principal holiday camp is at Seaton Valley. From the beach on a clear day there is a good view of the Eddystone Lighthouse. *Nearest town, bus depot and station—Liskeard.*

FALMOUTH (pop. 17,883) is the largest Cornish port and also one of the larger and more popular holiday resorts on the A39 (see page 58). There are four beaches and all resort amenities. *Bus services link Falmouth with Truro, Penryn, Helston, Redruth and surrounding areas; Passenger ferry to St. Mawes and Roseland; Information Bureaux; Prince of Wales Pier and Resort Manager's Office, Gyllyngvase Beach; Early closing day—Wednesday; Nearest mainline station— Truro (branch to Falmouth).*

FEOCK (pop. 2157) is an attractive riverside village near the A39 between Truro and Falmouth. The church of St. Feock, almost entirely rebuilt about 1874 has a detached bell tower. Trelissick Gardens (B3289), form a National Trust park, planted in the 1820s with fine rhododendrons, camellias and subtropical shrubs and superb views over the Carrick Roads. The gardens (only) are open from March to October, weekdays 10 a.m.–6 p.m., Sundays 2 p.m.–6 p.m. A 580 bus from Truro stops at Feock Fourturnings within about 1½ km (1 mile) of the lodge gates. At King Harry there is a passage or crossing (car ferry) to Philleigh in the Rose-

land peninsula. Thatched houses and cottages abound. In the nearby hamlet of Come-to-Good, the 18th century thatched Meeting House of the Society of Friends (the Quakers) is said to be the oldest such chapel in the country. A Shell/National Trust Nature Trail starts at Trelissick. *The nearest beach is Looe Beach; Nearest station—Truro.*

Thatched Cottages, Church Cove, Lizard

FLUSHING is a small village with a waterfront looking across the Penryn River or creek to Falmouth with which it is linked by regular passenger ferry. *Nearest town, bus depot and station—Penryn (Falmouth branch line from Truro).*

FOWEY (pop. 2300) is a south coast seaport, resort (holiday centre) reached by the B3269 from the A390 (see page 48) and is on the bus route. *Early closing day—Wednesday; Information Bureau—4 South Street; Nearest station—St. Austell.*

GULVAL is a pretty village on the outskirts of Penzance (B3311). The Ding Dong Mine is the oldest in Cornwall. Mead, a traditional drink is made locally. Near here is Chysauster, an ancient settlement which claims to possess visible remains of the oldest village street in England—between 1st and 2nd century BC and is well worth visiting. *Nearest town, beaches, bus depot and station—Penzance.*

GWENNAP (pop. 1095) is a large, scattered and somewhat barren parish with a 'churchtown' on the B3298 off the A393 between Falmouth and Redruth. John Wesley used to preach at Gwennap Pit, an amphitheatre with seats for 2000 people. Well attended Methodist meetings are traditionally held here on Whit-Monday (now the Spring Bank Holiday). *Nearest town, bus depot and station—Redruth.*

GWINEAR—GWITHIAN (pop. 2000) is a curious Cornish amalgam. Gwinear, inland, is a 'churchtown'. Gwithian on the B3301 coast road is also a 'churchtown' and so there are two separate communities in one parish. There are many good caravan and chalet parks as well as camping sites. Excellent beaches are to be found at Godrevy and Gwithian Towans. *Nearest town, bus depot and station—Hayle.*

HAYLE (pop. 6050) is a town on the A30, 11 km (7 miles) east of Penzance, and on the Carnsew Estuary. On a bus route, with a main line railway station, it is recommended as a touring centre (see page 63). There are excellent caravanning and camping sites in the locality, and a major feature is the 5 km (3 miles) of golden sands at Hayle Towans. *Early closing day—Thursday.*

HELSTON (pop. 6750) is the principal town of the Lizard Peninsula, and a touring centre on the A394 (see page 59) and is a centre for bus services. There is an interesting museum and good holiday accommodation facilities. The nearest beaches are at Gunwalloe, Poldhu, Mullion Cove and Porthleven. *Early closing day— Wednesday; Information Office— Council Office, The Willows, Church Street; Market days—Saturday and (cattle) Monday; Nearest station— Camborne.*

KEA (pop. 1625) is a scattered parish with several centres of population, the main one being Carnon Downs on the A39 Truro– Falmouth road. At Come-to-Good there is a picturesque meeting house of the Society of Friends (the Quakers) with a thatched roof and stabling (see Feock). *Nearest town, bus depot and station—Truro.*

KILKHAMPTON (pop. 700) is a most attractive village on the A39 dominated by the tall tower of St. James parish church. The church contains a Father Willis organ with the black and white keys reversed. The Tamar Lake is 5 km (3 miles) away and there are beaches at Sandymouth and Duckpool. The beautiful Coombe Valley, through which there is an interesting Nature Trail, belongs to the National Trust. *Nearest town and bus depot— Bude; Nearest station—Exeter (St. Davids).*

LANDEWEDNACK (pop. 750) (the Lizard Town) A3083 is the most southerly parish in the British Isles. The Lizard Light, Kilcobben Cove, and Marconi's Wireless Station, the Lifeboat and Lloyds Signal Station at Bass Point are reminders that this is an outpost, there is nothing beyond but the open sea, and communications, especially in times of distress, are all important. At Kynance Cove can be seen the unique cliffs of serpentine, that much prized and colourful rock formation. There are many craft shops where the serpentine is fashioned into souvenirs. *Nearest town and bus depot—Helston. Nearest station—Camborne.*

LANHYDROCK is an estate parish just outside Bodmin. The impressive Lanhydrock House (National Trust property) and adjacent parish church are well worth visiting. The house is open afternoons from April to October. *Nearest town and bus depot—Bodmin; Nearest station—Bodmin Road.*

LANIVET (pop. 1086) is a village on the A30 some 5 km (3 miles) west of Bodmin. This rural parish contains many interesting crosses and standing stones eg Reperry Cross. *Nearest town and bus depot—Bodmin; Nearest station—Bodmin Road.*

Kynance Cove

LANREATH is an interesting little village just off the B3359 which is the main approach road to Looe. There is an interesting church, a nice village inn under the sign of 'The Punchbowl', and Trevollard Farm Museum is authentic and worth visiting. *Nearest town, bus depot and station—Liskeard.*

LAUNCELLS is a tiny 'church-town' just visible from the A3072 Holsworthy–Bude road and is famous for its unrestored parish church of St. Swithin. *Nearest town and bus depot—Bude.*

LAUNCESTON (pop. 4779) on the A30 is the 'Gateway to Cornwall' and a touring centre (see page 42) is on the bus route. This inland town has many interesting buildings and features. *Early closing day—Thursday; Market Day—Tuesday; Information Office—Council Offices, Western Road; Cornwall Tourist Board Accommodation and Information Bureau—Lewdown. Nearest station—Plymouth (North Road).*

LINKINHORNE (pop. 1075) is a scattered moorland parish near the B3257 with a number of settlements or villages. There is an impressive number of interesting places to visit including the parish church, the Cheesewring, St. Melor's Holy Well, the Hurlers (stone monoliths) and old mine workings at Caradon Hill and Phoenix. *Nearest town, bus depot and station—Liskeard.*

LISKEARD (pop. 4482) is at the junction of the A38 (from the Tamar Bridge) and the 1390 over Gunnislake Bridge through Callington. It is a touring centre (see page 49) and is on bus routes and the main railway line. The Tremar Potteries may be visited and there are riding stables at Tokenbury Manor, Pensilva, and a Forest Miniature (Steam) Railway at Penmount, Dobwalls. *The nearest beaches are at Looe; Early closing—Wednesday; Market days—Monday and Thursday.*

LOOE (pop. 4050) on the A387 is really two towns in one, East Looe and West Looe linked by a seven-arched bridge over the river Looe (see page 46). There is much of interest here and good holiday accommodation of all types exists in the area. *Early closing—Thursday; Nearest main line station—Liskeard (branch to Looe); Information Bureau—Guildhall, East Looe;*

Cornwall Tourist Board Accommodation and Information Bureau—Heskyn Hill (A38).

LOSTWITHIEL (pop. 1900) is a rural borough and former stannary town on the A390 and the main railway line at the head of the navigable portion of the River Fowey. The ruins of Restormel Castle, built in the reign of Edward I, after which the new Borough which comprises mid-Cornwall is named, dominate the landscape. It was once the residence of the Earls of Cornwall and since 1300 the castle has been attached to the Duchy of Cornwall. Now in the care of the Department of the Environment it can be visited during daylight hours. The name Lostwithiel derives from 'Les' or 'Lis', a court, hall or palace 'Uchel' meaning high 'the high court' (of the Duke of Cornwall). The church of St. Bartholemew is an interesting building with an octagonal lantern tower. Downstream is the picturesque riverside church of St. Winnow with its Georgian vicarage close by and about 1½ km (1 mile) inland is the rural village of St. Veep noteworthy for its six bells which were cast in the 18th century as a 'virgin peal'—ie in perfect consonance without needing tuning. The popular and attractive riverside village of Lerryn is also in this parish. *The nearest beaches are at Fowey and Par; Early closing days—Wednesday and Saturday.*

LUDGVAN (pop. 2000) is a village and parish near Penzance on the B3309. There is an interesting old church and Tren Crom Hill on the parish boundary is worth climbing for the view. The nearest beach is at Marazion. *Nearest town, bus depot and station—Penzance.*

LUXULYAN (pop. 1012) is an inland village chiefly noteworthy for the magnificent wooded valley of the same name through which it is possible to drive and through which the Par-Newquay railway branch still runs, built last century by Squire Treffry of Prideaux House, Luxulyan. The house and Treffry's wonderful aqueduct across the valley can still be seen as can the ancient well or baptistry and Churchtown. *Nearest town and bus depot—St. Austell; Nearest station —Luxulyan (on branch line from Par).*

MADRON (pop. 1422) is another of the villages around Penzance. The parish contains some interesting relics including the famous Lanyon Quoit or Cromlech, the Men an Tol and Men Stryfa as well as the National Trust Gardens of Trengwainton. In the churchyard there is a Bapistry and Wishing Well. Each year on the nearest Sunday to Trafalgar Day (21st October) a ceremony is held to commemorate the fact that Penzance was the first town to receive the news of the Battle of Trafalgar in 1805 and the death of Lord Nelson. On the following Sunday the Mayor and Corporation walked in procession to the memorial service at Madron (which was then the Mother Church of Penzance) carrying the canvas banner which is now kept in the church and still carried at the anniversary services. The nearest beach is at Marazion. *Nearest bus depot, railway station and heliport— Penzance; Early closing day— Thursday.*

MANACCAN is one of the small villages that make up the district known as Meneage, in the Lizard Peninsula. There is a fig tree growing from the church wall and superstition has it that anyone who harms it in any way will meet a violent death. *The two nearest beaches are St. Anthony and at Gillan Creek on the Helford River; The nearest market town and bus depot—Helston.*

MARAZION (pop. 1500) is a town through which one approaches Penzance on the A394 from Helston. From the visitor's point of view it is to all intents and purposes part of the Penzance holiday area, but its residents like to preserve their independence. The town's first Charter was granted as far back as 1595 by Queen Elizabeth I. Marazion is noted as the oldest town in England in the (current) Guinness Book of Records, its name in Roman times being ICTIS. Neighbouring Penzance's principal street is called 'Market Jew Street'— another form of Marazion. The splendid beaches and the close proximity of St. Michael's Mount add to the attractions of Marazion which is a good centre for sailing (the local Sailing Club's Headquarters are at Godolphin Steps). It is served by buses from Helston and Penzance. *Early closing day— Wednesday.*

MARHAMCHURCH is an interesting village just off the A39 south of Bude. The parish church of St. Marwenne contains the Royal Arms of Charles II. The village revels are held on the Monday following the 12th August. *Nearest town and bus depot—Bude.*

MENHENIOT (pop. 1193) is a delightful little inland village clearly visible from the A38 Plymouth– Liskeard road, the spire of the parish church being a landmark. Blackaton Rings are earthworks in the parish and there are roadstone quarries at Clicker Tor. *Nearest town, bus depot and station—Liskeard (some trains also stop at Menheniot).*

MEVAGISSEY (pop. 2000) is a fishing port and together with neighbouring Portmellon forms a holiday centre on the B3273 (see page 49). There is a Folk Museum, a model railway and an interesting Aquarium. Boat trips and fishing expeditions are numerous and recommended. *Information Office— Post Office (St. George's Square); Nearest town, bus depot, station and motorail terminal—St. Austell.*

MORVAH is a tiny village near the coast road B3306 between St. Just and St. Ives. The church and village now stand off the main road. Many relics of the past including Chun Quoit on Chun Downs and Chun Castle are to be found in this wind-swept and rather barren parish. The remains of Cornwall's oldest mine workings, the Ding Dong Mine can still be seen between Penzance and Morvah. *Nearest town, bus depot, station and heliport—Penzance.*

MORWENSTOW (pop. 523) is the most northerly of the parishes of Cornwall. The church stands in a most exposed cliffside position close to the old Vicarage which has miniature church towers as its principal chimneys. This feature was one of the eccentricities of Robert Stephen Hawker the parson-poet, Vicar of Morwenstow from 1834 to 1875. Hawker's Hut, his solitary retreat on the cliff top, can still be visited. Tonnacombe House built about the year 1500 is an interesting feature of this rather bleak, but

Life-boat

nonetheless attractive part of North Cornwall. *The nearest town and bus depot—Bude. Nearest station— Exeter (St. David's).*

MOUSEHOLE (pop. 1093) is a small fishing community near Penzance. Its chief attraction lies in its picturesque harbour which has been painted by scores of artists, and which is extremely popular with visitors. Mousehole was burned by the Spaniards in 1595 and only one building is said to have survived, the then inn called the Keigwin Arms. Today this building is a private house but the striking exterior with an overhanging first floor over the front porch can still be admired. *Nearest bus depot, railway station and Heliport—Penzance.*

MULLION (pop. 1300) is a village with a delightful little harbour and the famous Mullion Cove on the bus route from Helston. The soft golden sands at Poldhu, Polurrian and Mullion Cove are extremely popular with visitors and there are good caravanning and camping as well as hotel, guest house and bed & breakfast facilities in this locality. Poldhu is noteworthy because it was from here that Marconi sent the first transatlantic wireless signal and the Marconi Monument can be seen on Poldhu Cliffs. The parish church contains some fine bench ends. *The nearest bus depot and market town is at Helston; Early closing day— Wednesday.*

MYLOR (pop. 2372) The pretty village of Mylor Bridge stands at the head of Mylor Creek, which is really the intersection of the Restronguet and Penryn Creeks. It is served by buses, and road access is off the A39 near Perranarworthal. From the waterfront, where the picturesque church of St. Melorus stands amid the wooded surroundings, literally

hundreds of boats of all sizes carry sailing enthusiasts all over this large area of landlocked waterway. Amateur sailors however should be very careful as south-easterly gales can whip up the estuary's usually calm waters into a frenzy and inside the little church the memorial to those lost when the Darlwin sank in 1966 is a poignant reminder of the perils of the deep. *Nearest towns, bus depots and railway stations— Truro and Falmouth.*

NEWLYN (pop. 3373) is well known for its artists community as well as its picturesque harbour and busy fish quay. Here also are the Tremaen Pottery and several art galleries including the Passmore Edwards Gallery which can be visited. Newlyn for all its quaintness and charm is a bustling place and is a vital part of the holiday area centred on Penzance. Newlyn has a history and in 1598 it too suffered by being burnt down by the Spaniards. Penzance is adjacent for all transport facilities.

NEWQUAY (pop. 13,200) is undoubtedly Cornwall's premier seaside resort, boasting no less than nine beaches in addition to the usual amenities expected in a large holiday centre (see page 30). Newquay is reached by rail (change at Par), by air (Newquay Air Terminal, St. Mawgan R.A.F. Station) and of course by road A3058 from A30 Summercourt, A392 from A30 Indian Queens or A3059 from A39 St. Columb Major. *Early closing day—Wednesday; Accommodation Bureau—Morfa Hall, Cliff Road; Information Office—Municipal Offices, Marcus Hill.*

PADSTOW (pop. 2113) (A389 or B3274 off A39) is a delightful seaport town on the western side of the estuary of the River Camel. Its harbour, sailing and boating facilities and its nearness to many beaches recommend it as a holiday centre as described on page 28. *Early closing day—Wednesday; Nearest station—Bodmin Road (bus link via Wadebridge).*

PAUL is a small village 5 km (3 miles) from Penzance. An interesting monument by the churchyard wall commemorates Dorothy or Dolly Pentreath, reputed to be the last person to speak the ancient or true Cornish language, who died in 1778 at the age of 102. The monument was erected in 1860 by Prince Louis Lucien Bonaparte and the then vicar, Revd. John Garrett. *Nearest town, bus depot and railway station—Penzance.*

PENRYN (pop. 5330). Penryn became a municipal borough in 1216, long before its more affluent neighbour, Falmouth, thus creating rivalry between the two places. Although Penryn has the advantage, historically, and is still a place of some commercial importance, it must feel it has been rather left behind. Far too many properties seem neglected but even so there are some features of interest to the casual visitor. The Town Hall in the centre of Market Street was built in 1625, but has an early Victorian addition, beneath which there is a most interesting museum. Penryn was an important ecclesiastical centre in medieval times and the monks of Glasney College were renowned for their scholarship. Remains of the College can still be traced in College Hill and St. Thomas Street. Penryn has a busy waterfront with good anchorages and moorings for boats of all descriptions. *Bus services link Penryn to neighbouring towns, and it has its own halt on the branch railway line from Truro to Falmouth;*

Information   Office—Municipal Offices;   Early   closing   day— Thursday.

PENZANCE (pop. 19,064) is a market town of considerable size and importance literally at the end of the line—it being the terminus of the Western Region railway line from Paddington, and the last major town of the A30 trunk road. There is also a motorail terminal. It is more fully described as a holiday and touring centre on page 65. *Nearest beach—Marazion; Early closing day—Wednesday; Cattle Market each Tuesday, with Thursday and Saturday being regarded as the 'other' market days; Information Office—Alverton—opposite the Guildhall.*

PERRANARWORTHAL (pop. 1261) is a village, part of which lies along the main A39 road between Truro and Falmouth. The well known Norway Inn, by the main road, derives its name from the fact that centuries ago long-boats were able to bring Norwegian timber for shoring up the mine workings upriver as far as Perran Wharf. Surprisingly enough Perran Wharf also had an important foundry which supplied the mines. Old Williams Perran Foundry, as it is called, can still be visited. A 20th century association remains at Tullimar House (also on the main Truro–Falmouth road) where General Eisenhower had his headquarters prior to D-Day, June 6th 1944. Allied troops from many nations embarked for Normandy from the estuaries and creeks of the River Fal. *The village is served by buses on the Truro—Falmouth route. Nearest towns, bus depots and railway stations—Truro and Falmouth.*

PERRANPORTH (pop. 2162) is a holiday resort on the B3285 off A30 at Boxheater Cross (see page 61) and is on the bus route. It is famous for its beach, and holiday accommodation of all types is plentiful and good. *Nearest station—Truro; Early closing day—Wednesday.*

PILLATON is a delightful village in the lovely valley of the River Lynher, a few miles south of Callington. The church of St. Odulph is hard by 'The Weary Friar', a notable inn with a reputation for good food. *Nearest market town, bus depot and station—Liskeard.*

POLPERRO (pop. 1250) is usually associated with its larger neighbour, Looe, in terms of coach trips and guide books. Polperro however is essentially a place on its own—a picturesque little fishing village, the centre of the parish of Lansallos. Fishing boats can still be seen in the harbour and although most of the village has been given over to tourism, it, nevertheless, still has much to charm the eye. Formerly the haunt of smugglers, their era is recreated in the contents of the Smugglers Museum and one can easily imagine the comings and goings of an earlier age as one looks at the House on the Props, the Old Watch House, the Old Bark House and the Saxon and Roman Bridges

to mention just a few of Polperro's seemingly ageless and endless delights. A Shell House and model village are also on the list of Polperro's tourist attractions. There is a wide variety of accommodation in the neighbourhood but possibly Polperro suffers from being a place of the day-trippers. Traffic is normally banned from the narrow streets and this helps the pedestrian. On the outskirts is Sclerder Abbey, a Roman Catholic community. *The nearest market town is Liskeard; Nearest station—Liskeard; Early closing day—Saturday.*

POLZEATH is a resort village at the centre of a popular holiday area (see page 27) on the north coast reached by the B3267 and B3314 from A39. There is a good beach and holiday accommodation of all types is plentiful. *Early closing day —Wednesday; Information Bureau —Coronation Gardens; Nearest town and bus depot—Wadebridge; Nearest station—Bodmin Road.*

PORT ISAAC (pop. 831) is a charming fishing village off the B3314 coast road from A39. This is part of the Polzeath and Camel Coast holiday area (see page 27). An attractive rock-strewn beach is at Port Gaverne. *Nearest market*

Polperro Harbour

town and bus depot—Wadebridge;
Nearest station—Bodmin Road.

PORTHLEVEN (pop. 3022) is an
attractive little seaport forming part
of the former Borough of Helston.
It has a small harbour from which a
few fishing boats still put to sea.
Accommodation can be obtained in
and around Porthleven but chiefly
this is a place for a half-day visit
when one can absorb the atmosphere, walk or drive along the
coast and perhaps picnic in sight of
Loe Pool and Bar. *Nearest town
and bus depot—Helston.*

POUNDSTOCK (pop. 700) is a
roadside village on the A39 west of
Bude. The churchtown with a
church and medieval Guildhouse
is a short distance down a narrow
country road. The fine beach of
Widemouth Bay is in this parish.
Nearest town and bus depot—Bude.

PROBUS (pop. 1492) is a compact
village on the A390 and bus route
between St. Austell and Truro. The
fine gardens of the 18th-century
Trewithen House are open to the
public, as also is the County
Education Committee's Demonstra-
tion Garden. For the gardening
enthusiast there are permanent
demonstrations of garden practices,
garden design and maintenance
etc. There is also an arboretum of
ornamental trees. The Garden is
open on Thursdays 2 p.m.–8 p.m.
and Sundays 2 p.m.–6 p.m. between
May and September and on Thursdays 2 p.m.–5 p.m. October to
April. The Church of SS Probus
and Grace is an interesting building
and its 36 m (120 ft) high tower is
regarded as the finest in Cornwall.
Nearest station—Truro.

RAME HEAD and the surrounding
countryside and seaboard. The
most south-easterly part of Cornwall

is made up of several attractive
inland and small coastal villages,
such as Kingsand, Cawsand, Millbrook and St. John. The beaches
are mostly shingle, as is usually
found on the south coast, but there
are good sailing and boating
facilities. Farmhouse accommodation is also available and represents
good value for money. The imposing Portwrinkle Hotel was brought
brick by brick from Plymouth and
enjoys a superb situation overlooking Whitesand Bay, and St. Johns'
Inn is over 500 years old. The great
open space of Mount Edgcumbe
Country Park is now open to the
public, some 30 hectares (74 acres)
having been purchased jointly by
Cornwall County Council and
Plymouth City Council. The house
is sometimes open to the public, and
from the grounds magnificent views
of the channel, Plymouth Sound
and the Hamoaze can be obtained.
The Holy Well of St. Julien at
Maker is of interest to the antiquarian as is the Chapel of St.
Michael on Rame Head. Fort
Tregantle occupies a commanding
position on the promontory and
from its lower slopes one can watch
the ships of the Royal Navy
entering or leaving the Royal Dock-
yard at Devonport.

REDRUTH (pop. 10,352) is the
eastern partner of the Camborne–
Redruth industrial area and suggested touring centre (see page 63).
It has a bus depot and main line
railway station. *Early closing day—
Thursday; Market day—Friday.*

ROCHE (pop. 1737) is an exposed
village on the edge of both the Goss
Moor and the china-clay area. Its
chief landmark is Roche Rock, a
granite outcrop which appears,
completely out of context, to the
east of the village (off the B3274).
On top of this stony mass are the

ruins of a hermit's or anchorite's cell and chapel (dedicated to St. Michael). *Roche is served by buses on the St. Austell–Newquay route; Nearest town, bus depot and railway station—St. Austell.*

ROCK is a resort village forming part of the Camel Coast holiday area. There is a sandy foreshore and the estuary provides good boating facilities. Holiday accommodation of all types is plentiful. *Information Bureau—Coronation Gardens. Polzeath; Nearest town and bus depot—Wadebridge; Nearest station—Bodmin Road; Passenger ferry to Padstow.*

ST. AGNES (pop. 4714) on the B3285 and bus routes is a town increasing in popularity as a holiday centre. Once a mining and fishing village, St. Agnes has a long and colourful history and evidence of this can be seen in the ruined mine-stacks that surround St. Agnes Beacon (a splendid vantage point and a good place for a summer picnic) and in the traces of the piers that were built in 1714 and 1794 at Trevaunance. On St. Agnes Head are the romantic ruins of Wheal Coates mine, now the property of the National Trust. Stippy-Stappy, a steep 'stepped' row of slate-roofed cottages are among the charms of St. Agnes which has good beaches literally on its doorstep. Tourist amenities and facilities for recreation are increasing in this area where a comparatively new model village is becoming well established. *Nearest station—Truro.*

ST. ANTHONY IN MENEAGE is really not much more than a creek-side hamlet or 'churchtown' at the head of Gillan Creek reached by road from the B3293 from Helston. The attractive interior of St. Anthony's church is worth looking

at, and its romantic situation near a shingle beach is most attractive. Coneysburrow Cliff and Herra, both at Gillan, are superb stretches of coastline, open for all to enjoy as the land belongs to the National Trust. *Nearest market town and bus depot—Helston.*

ST. ANTHONY IN ROSELAND tends largely to be forgotten as it is well off the beaten track lying as it does off the A3078 Truro–St. Mawes road, on an inlet of the Percuil River, in the Roseland peninsula. Apart from St. Anthony lighthouse on Zoze Point, St. Anthony's principal attraction is its church and adjoining manor house. The church, one of the best Early English churches in Cornwall was restored last century. It has a central tower and spire, a richly carved Norman south door and a number of imposing monuments to the Spry Family who lived at Place, a neo-Gothic house grafted on to the church. Built in 1840 the house stands on the site of the former priory buildings associated with the monks of Plympton. The Old Rectory is now part of the house. *Nearest town, bus depot and station—Truro.*

ST. AUSTELL (pop. 13,500) an important commercial and industrial centre is included as a suggested touring centre (see page 51). St. Austell is the capital of the china-clay countryside and the centre of the industry, but beaches at Carlyon Bay, Porthpean and Charlestown are within easy reach. Road and rail (including Motorail) communications between St. Austell and other parts of Cornwall as well as outside the country are good. *Information Office — Municipal Offices, Truro Road; Early closing day—Thursday; Market days—Tuesday and Friday.*

ST. BREWARD (pop. 749) is a windswept, rather bare moorland village just off the B3266 on the edge of Bodmin Moor. Here are the great granite quarries of Hantergantick and De Lank, as well as many prehistoric antiquities. Cornwall's highest peaks Rough Tor, 400 m (1311 ft) and Brown Willy, 419 m (1375 ft) are also in the parish. *Nearest town and bus depot— Wadebridge; Nearest station—Bodmin Road.*

ST. BURYAN (pop. 976) is a somewhat isolated village whose tall church tower dominates the unusually flat surrounding landscape of this part of the Lands End peninsula. The ancient stone circle called the Merrymaidens and the cross called Crows-an-Wra are among the antiquities of this parish. It is however Lamorna Cove which attracts the tourists and the artists and there is also easy access to Penberth Cove and Penberth Valley from St. Buryan. *Nearest town, railway station and bus depot— Penzance.*

ST. CLEER (pop. 2000) is very definitely a moorland village, dominated by the noble tower of the parish church which can be seen for many miles across the moors. The Holy Well has a granite canopy. Just outside the village is the massive Trethevy Quoit and, on a roadside site carefully laid out by the Liskeard Old Cornwall Society, are two massive monoliths known as King Doniert's Stones, reputedly marking the burial place of Doniert, the last of the Cornish Kings. *Nearest market town, bus depot and railway station—Liskeard.*

ST. COLUMB MAJOR (pop. 3441) is a small market town and parish on the A39 at the head of the Vale of Lanherne. It is therefore a good touring centre (see page 37) from which to visit almost the entire Atlantic coast with central and south Cornwall also being within easy reach. *Nearest main line station —Bodmin Road or St. Austell; Nearest station—St. Columb Road (Par-Newquay Branch Line); Nearest airport—Newquay (R.A.F. St. Mawgan); Market day—Monday; Early closing day—Wednesday.*

ST. DAY (pop. 1184) is a former mining town which suffered a serious depression a century ago and has not recovered until the 1970s. Situated off the main traffic routes between A30 and A393 east of Redruth, it overlooks a rather desolate and forlorn part of the old Mining Division, although particularly in spring and early summer, a drive through this rather remote part of inland Cornwall can be a rewarding and interesting experience. *Nearest town, bus depot and station—Redruth.*

ST. DOMINICK (pop. 633) is one of the horticultural village communities in the fertile Tamar Valley, just off the A388, south of Callington. The area is noted for early flowers, vegetables and fruit, especially strawberries. Halton Quay on the River Tamar is interesting and there is a riding school at Trelill.

ST. ENDELLION (pop. 1052) is a parish with a 'churchtown' on the B3314. Port Isaac is a fishing village within the parish. The St. Endellion Music Festival, held each July in the collegiate church of St. Endelienta, is an important event. *Nearest town and bus depot— Wadebridge; Nearest station—Bodmin Road.*

ST. ERTH (pop. 896) is a village just off the A30, best known as the rail junction for St. Ives, but deserving to be known in its own right by those interested in relics of bygone ages. There is, for example, a 14th-century bridge over the river Hayle, at Bosenee, Roman remains are contained in an earthwork and Trelowth Farm has an interesting two-storeyed porch. Parts of Trewinnard Manor House date from the 17th century and numerous ancient stone crosses exist in the parish. *Early closing day—Thursday; Nearest towns, bus depots and stations—Camborne or Penzance.*

ST. GENNYS is a north coastal parish not far from Bude containing the charming little seaside village of Crackington Haven where there is a beach. *Nearest town and bus depot—Bude.*

ST. GERMANS (pop. 1962) is a village which has several notable features and those who turn off the main roads (A38 or A374) on either side will find their detour or bus journey worthwhile. From the year A.D. 931, when after his conquest of Cornwall, Althelstan built a church on the site of a Celtic church founded in the 5th century by St. Germanus, this was the seat of the see or Diocese of Cornwall. In 1030 the Bishopric was removed to Crediton and subsequently to Exeter, where it remained until 1877 when the Diocese of Truro was formed. Towards the end of the 12th century the church was again rebuilt in the Norman style and so it remains to this day with its splendid Norman doorway and two western towers. Port Eliot, the seat of the Earl of St. Germans is a large mansion on the site of the ancient priory close to the church. The 12 almshouses erected by one of the Moyle family are also of interest. *Nearest station—St. Germans (not all trains stop); Nearest main line station—Plymouth (North Road).*

ST. IVE (pop. 1544) is a roadside village on the A390 Liskeard–Callington road. The famous Cornish Bishop Jonathan Trelawney is listed as a former Vicar. *Nearest town, bus depot and station—Liskeard.*

ST. IVES (pop. 7012) is probably one of the best known holiday centres in Great Britain, quite apart from Cornwall. Ideally situated on the western arm of St. Ives Bay it has good beaches, holiday accommodation facilities and amenities. Road and rail communications are good (see page 64). *Thursday is normally early-closing day. Nearest station—St. Ives (branch line from St. Erth).*

ST. JUST (pop. 3500) is the largest town in the immediate vicinity of the Land's End Peninsula. St. Just was once a most important mining centre with the Botallack, Geevor and Levant mines on its outskirts. Botallack mine ran out under the sea for about 550 m (600 yd), and Levant, the scene of a great disaster in 1911, extended some 3 km (2 miles) under the sea. St. Just is an attractive place with some very fine buildings in the triangular town centre. Beside Bank Square is an amphitheatre—the Plain-an-Gwarry or Playing Place, where plays and other entertainments took place in medieval times. The outstanding natural features include the massive promontory of Cape Cornwall, Carn Gloose, Chapel Carn Brea (National Trust Property) just off the B3306, Carn Kenidjack on the north side of the town and Chun Quoit towards Morvah. Throughout the district, holiday accommodation of every kind exists in plenty, and if one decides to stay in or near St. Just, in addition to the delights of exploring the surrounding country-side, there are several beaches close at hand at Boat Cove, Porthledden, Priests Cove, Penaven and Gwenver. Light aircraft take off on pleasure flights from the little grass-covered airstrip. *Nearest station, bus depots and heliport—Penzance.*

ST. JUST IN ROSELAND on the A3078 is the mother parish of the Roseland peninsula and has St. Mawes as one of her children. The chief attraction of the village is the uniquely beautiful situation of the 12th-century church of St. Just, right on the water's edge. The superbly kept churchyard and the church itself attract thousands of visitors each year. *There is a bus service to Truro; Nearest market town, bus depot and station—Truro.*

ST. KEVERNE (pop. 1765) is a village at the centre of the Lizard Peninsula and of an essentially farming area, which provides a focal point for several scattered communities. Places of interest and beauty in the vicinity include Porthallow, Zoar, Ponsongath and Coverack. *Nearest market town and bus depot—Helston.*

ST. KEW (pop. 831) is a superbly set village, not far off the A39, in the hinterland of the Polzeath holiday area. The church of St. Kewa is an interesting building with some good stained glass. At Pendoggett the famous Cornish Arms hostelry is noted for its good food and another good inn is the Maltsters Arms, in the nearby village of Chapel Amble. *Nearest town and bus depot—Wadebridge; Nearest station—Bodmin Road.*

ST. KEYNE is a small village on the B3254 between Liskeard and Looe, situated in an attractive wooded valley. There is a famous wayside

Fishing-boats in St. Ives Harbour

well, dedicated in the name of St. Keyne, which is supposed to possess mystical properties in that of husband and wife, whoever drinks first of its waters after their marriage will be master of the other. At St. Keyne Mill can also be seen the rare and intriguing collection of musical automata assembled by Mr. Paul Corin. During the summer season (May–September) the museum is open 10.30 a.m.–1.00 p.m., 2.30 p.m.–5.00 p.m. and 6.30 p.m.–8.30 p.m. and during the rest of the year it is open on Saturdays and Sundays 2.30 p.m.–5.00 p.m. *Nearest market town, bus depot and main line station—Liskeard.*

ST. LEVAN is a small and rather remote village, but is one to which most visitors to West Cornwall who drive along the B3283 find their way at some time or other. There is a good beach at Porthcurno and nearby is the unique open air Minack Theatre. Productions are staged during the summer months and programmes are readily available at local information centres during the season. Penberth in Penberth Cove, an original fishing village, is now owned by the National Trust. The Logan Stone at Treen is a famous rocking stone. *Nearest town, bus depot and station—Penzance.*

ST. MAWES (pop. 852) is the principal village of the Roseland peninsula and is a recommended holiday centre (see page 57). Holiday accommodation and facilities are plentiful and there are good beaches in the vicinity. *Nearest station—Truro.*

ST. MAWGAN-IN-PYDAR (pop. 986) is without doubt one of the loveliest of the Cornish villages, superbly set in a deep valley (the vale of Lanherne) off A3059 (St.

Columb–Newquay), through which the Menalhyl river flows peacefully from St. Columb to the sea at Mawgan Porth. Time seems to stand still in St. Mawgan as one surveys the lofty 14th-century tower of the granite church hard by Lanherne, the old manor-house of the Arundells. Since 1794 Lanherne has been the home of a community of Carmelite nuns who sought refuge at the time of the French Revolution. In the churchyard there is a 13th-century lantern cross and in the convent grounds is an even earlier cross, probably dating from the 10th century. Almshouses and the fascinating Falcon Inn, so re-named when the Arundell family and other recusants were being persecuted for their faith, a falcon was released as a signal that a priest was about to say Mass at some secret place. A village school and an arched bridge complete what, even in the 20th century, is still a very tranquil picture. Although the roar of aircraft from St. Mawgan R.A.F. station less than 1½ km (1 mile) away, on the high ground above the village near the great house of Carnanton sometimes intrudes on this tranquillity. St. Mawgan is on a bus route. There are beaches at Mawgan Porth, Trenance and Watergate Bay. *Nearest market town—St. Columb; Nearest airport—Newquay (R.A.F. St. Mawgan); Nearest station—Newquay (Branch from Par).*

ST. MICHAEL CAERHAYES is a charming little seaside village in the Roseland Peninsula. Here is Caerhayes Castle, the gardens of which are usually open on two occasions in the year, and there are beaches at Porthluney and East Portholland. *Nearest town, bus depot and station—Truro.*

ST. NEOT (pop. 850) is very much

a moorland village and its superb situation just off Bodmin Moor makes it a must for visitors. The lovely church of St. Neot has a lantern cross in the churchyard and the finest examples of medieval stained glass in the county. An oak branch is placed on the top of the tower on 29th May every year by the men of the parish to commemorate King Charles II hiding in an oak tree to escape the Roundheads. Relics of the past abound in this large parish, including a holy well in Milltown Field in the Village itself. Dozmary Pool, the legendary resting place of Excalibur, the Sword of King Arthur, is 8 km (5 miles) away to the north and there is an ancient fort and hut circles on Bury Down to the north east of the village. A beauty spot is the pretty valley of the Loveny river, one of Cornwall's lesser known streams. One of the chief recreational attractions here and on the surrounding moors is pony-trekking and facilities exist at Northwood and Menaridden. *Nearest market town, bus depot and station—Liskeard.*

ST. NEWLYN EAST (pop. 1418) is a village at the centre of a triangle formed by three main roads, A30, A3075 and A3058, not far from Newquay. The National Trust property, Trerice Manor, is in the parish, as is the A30 roadside village of Mitchell, formerly a 'rotten' borough which once numbered Sir Walter Raleigh among its non-resident Members of Parliament.

ST. STEPHEN-IN-BRANNEL (pop. 4949) is the village centre of a large parish on the A3058. This comprises a number of villages forming part of the china-clay countryside and linked by a bus service from St. Austell to Newquay. *Nearest town, bus depot and station—St. Austell.*

ST. TUDY (pop. 450) Captain Bligh of the Bounty was born in this pleasant village which lies just off Bodmin Moor. Apart from an old church, it boasts an unusual Paperweight Centre and the gardens of Tremeer, the home of an authority on the growing of rhododendrons, azaleas and other shrubs, is open to the public at regular intervals. *Nearest towns and bus depots— Bodmin and Wadebridge; Nearest station—Bodmin Road.*

ST. WINWALLOE or Gunwalloe is a tiny village, almost on the beach, looking out over the wild sea, reached by car or bus from Helston. The parish church of St. Winwalloe, yet another of the almost unknown Celtic Saints, is one of the oldest in Cornwall and on three sides the walls and those of the little tower are formed of the solid rock against which it stands. A constant battle is fought to keep the sea from completely engulfing the little church. *Nearest town and bus depot— Helston.*

SALTASH (pop. 9608) is at the western end of the Tamar Bridge (A38), and is suggested as a centre from which to tour the Rame Peninsula (see page 55). *Early closing day—Wednesday; Nearest station—Saltash (for Plymouth North Road).*

SANCREED (pop. 548) is a small village just off the A30 about 8 km (5 miles) from Penzance. There are a number of interesting archaeological remains in the parish, including Chapel Euny, a Holy Well on Chapel Downs and some 'ancient digs' at Gold Herring. There is also an imposing and not unattractive reservoir at Drift. *Nearest town, bus depot, station and heliport—Penzance.*

SENNEN (pop. 700) is only a small village but it has the distinction of being the first and last parish in England, and it seems that everything else in the Lands End vicinity also carries that label. Thousands of visitors come here annually to gaze out across the Atlantic Ocean to the Wolf Rock and Longships Lighthouses, and on a clear day to dimly discern the Isles of Scilly 58 km (36 miles) away. Apart from the magic of Lands End there is also Sennen Cove, or really Whitesand Bay, one of the best known of Cornish beaches. There is also a little harbour and the lifeboat house and slipway are another reminder of stormy days when the services of the volunteer crew are needed to rescue those in danger. Near the tower of Sennen's ancient church is a stone cross probably well over a thousand years old, but apart from the antiquities of the place, Sennen is a very good place indeed around

which to spend a holiday. Accommodation of all kinds is plentiful and generally not too expensive. *Nearest town, bus depot, railway station and heliport—Penzance.*

STITHIANS (pop. 1600) is a pleasant village on the minor road and bus route between Penryn and Pool (near Camborne) with an ancient church. Stithians Show, held each mid-July, is a formidable assembly of things rural, agricultural, horticultural and culinary and is regarded as one of the leading shows in the county. Just outside the village is the Stithians Impounding Reservoir and Dam which supplies water for a large part of the area. *Nearest towns, bus depots and stations—Redruth and Camborne.*

STOKECLIMSLAND (pop. 1086) is a village just off the A388 to the north of Callington. Kit Hill overlooking Hingston Down is a famous

Quaint buildings on the slipway, Sennen

vantage point. *Nearest town and bus depot—Callington.*

STRATTON (pop. 1275), an ancient market town and the mother parish of the popular holiday resort of Bude, is well worth visiting for its historical associations as well as its charm. In 1643 a famous battle was fought at Stamford Hill, just outside the town, between Royalist forces commanded by a local hero, Sir Bevil Grenville and Cromwell's troops. Sir Bevil's faithful retainer, the almost legendary Cornish giant Antony Payne was 2·23 m (7 ft 4 in) tall, and when he died was placed in such a large coffin that it could not be removed from the manor house (now the Tree Inn in Stratton itself), until part of the floor had been cut away. The tall tower of the parish church of St. Andrew dominates the town. *Nearest town and bus depot—Bude; Nearest railway station—Exeter, St. David's.*

SUMMERCOURT (pop. 1479) on the A30 is the village nucleus of the scattered parish of St. Enoder. The main event of the year is Summercourt Fair held on 25th September, which attracts thousands of people and takes place on the main road (as well as in the Fair Park) causing a major traffic diversion. *Nearest town, bus depot, station and airport —Newquay.*

TINTAGEL (pop. 1300) is an attractive village and holiday centre on the north coast, B3263 (see page 26). The nearest beaches are at Trebarwith Strand, Castle Cove and Bossiney Cove. Tintagel is the focal point of Cornwall's 'King Arthur's Country' and there is much of interest in the locality. *Early closing day—Wednesday; Nearest town and bus depot—Camelford; Nearest station—Bodmin Road.*

TORPOINT (pop. 6320) is a town on the west bank of the river Tamar, immediately opposite Devonport to which it is linked by a regular ferry service. Antony House, on the road westwards out of Torpoint, is National Trust property and open two afternoons a week during the summer. It is the home of the Lord Lieutenant of Cornwall Col. Sir John Carew Pole (Bart). Although not a particularly attractive town, Torpoint is a good place from which to explore the Rame Peninsula (q.v.). *Early closing day—Wednesday; Nearest station—Plymouth, North Road.*

TREGONY (pop. 686) is on a bus route and at the junction of A3078 and B3287 and rightly regards itself as the gateway to the Roseland. Before the river silted up, Tregony was a place of considerable importance as evidenced by its 15th-century town hall, and 13th-century Almshouses. St. Cuby's church dates from the 15th century and there was a castle here between 1100 and 1500. Altogether an interesting place to visit, possibly en route for the other delights of the Roseland. *Nearest town, bus depot and station—Truro.*

TREVOSE HEAD and the surrounding beaches to the west of Padstow. Guarding the entrance to the Camel Estuary is formidable Trevose Head, once a menace to shipping. The lighthouse on the headland now guides vessels safely past the jagged rocks. A private toll road leads to the headland which provides a magnificent panorama of sky, sea and land. All around are found soft, sandy beaches which are simply ideal for surfing and lying in the sun. On the west bank of the River Camel, nearest to Padstow, come Mother Ivey's Bay and Booby's Bay, then nestling between

Stepper Point and Trevose Head itself is the attractive seaside village of Trevone with lovely Porthmizzen Beach. Facing the open ocean to the west of Trevose Head is Harlyn Bay, followed in rapid succession by Constantine, Treyarnon and Porthcothan, all within the large parish of St. Merryn, the village nucleus of this attractive holiday area. Evidence of early inhabitants of this part of Cornwall were unearthed, or rather unsanded, at Harlyn in 1900 when a prehistoric burial ground with some 27 slate coffins containing human skeletons was discovered. The relics can be seen at Harlyn Bay Museum. From Porthcothan it is but a short distance to Bedruthan Steps, so called because of the steep descent to the beach cut into the rock. Unfortunately these steps are no longer safe and access to the beach is prohibited. The cliff top walks in this area however are magnificent, especially early in the year when there is an abundance of wild flowers. Inland are the attractive villages of St. Issey and Little Petherick, and dominating the landscape, the tower of St. Eval church originally built by the Merchant Venturers of Bristol to warn their captains of the perils of this part of the coast in the days before Trevose Lighthouse was erected. St. Eval, its church and the surrounding area has also passed into more recent history. Many of the runways and buildings of the former original coastal command station can still be seen and the little church has been 'adopted' by the Royal Air Force now from across the valley at St. Mawgan. *Nearest towns and bus depots—Padstow or Wadebridge; Nearest station—Bodmin Road.*

TRURO (pop. 14,830) is the cathedral city and administrative capital of Cornwall. Its position at the junction of A39, A3076 and A390 makes it an important centre of road communication. It is also on the main Plymouth–Penzance line and is therefore suggested as a touring centre (see page 56 for description and tours routes). All the principal clearing banks have offices here. *(Cattle) Market day— Wednesday; Early closing day— Thursday.*

VERYAN (pop. 906) is a most attractive village set just off the A3078 amid wooded scenery in the Roseland peninsula. There are some good places to stay both in the village itself and the surrounding area. The open space of Mor Launder and the garden of the ancient church provide a tranquil village setting, but the real pride of the village is the four 'round houses'. These thatched cottages were built in the round to thwart the devil, who traditionally lurked in dark corners. Just for good measure the round houses also have crosses on the top. Portloe is a delightful little fishing village on the mouth of a small river with a pebbly beach but nice enough for a picnic or to sit and watch the boats. *Nearest town, bus depot and station—Truro.*

WADEBRIDGE (pop. 4000) is a market town on the A39 and bus routes. It is recommended as a touring centre (see page 35). The nearest beaches are in the Polzeath area and around Trevose Head. *Early closing day—Wednesday; Nearest station—Bodmin Road.*

WEEK ST. MARY is a small village south of Bude, lying between the A39 and B3254. It is chiefly noteworthy as the home of Thomasina Bonaventure who married three times, and became the wife of a Lord Mayor of London. Burdenwell

Manor in Lower Square is an interesting building probably dating from pre-Tudor times. *Nearest town and bus depot—Bude.*

WENDRON (pop. 2000) is the village centre of a large parish. On the B3297 and bus route from Redruth to Helston, one of its chief claims to fame nowadays is Wendron Forge where local craftsmen still employ traditional skills to produce souvenirs of high quality.
Nearest town and bus depot— Helston; Nearest station—Redruth.

ZENNOR is one of the fascinating villages on the B3306 coast road from Lands End to St. Ives. Mention has already been made of the Mermaid of Zennor—visitors should not fail to visit the parish church and see the famous medieval bench end. A wayside Folk Museum has been established here and is worth a brief visit. The principal attractions here, though, are for the antiquarians. Within a very short radius of Zennor village is Zennor Cromlech 2½ km (1½ miles); a Hut Circle 1½ km (1 mile); a medieval chapel 1½ km (1 mile); Barrows and burial chambers at nearby Treen, Zennor Quoit and an Iron Age Cliffcastle at Gurnard's Head—a fascinating list, which can provide hours of interest. *Nearest town, bus depot, railway station and heliport— Penzance.*

Mermaid Benchend, Zennor Church

Cornish food

INDEX

*All places which have a main entry, and the pages on
which these occur, are printed in heavy type.
The page numbers in colour are map references.
Asterisks indicate illustrations.*